FEMINIST READINGS OF
NATIVE AMERICAN LITERATURE

FEMINIST READINGS OF

NATIVE AMERICAN LITERATURE

Coming to Voice

Kathleen M. Donovan

The University of Arizona Press ~ Tucson

The University of Arizona Press
First printing

Versions of chapters of this book were previously published in *SAIL, a/b:Auto/ Biography Studies,* and *Native American Literatures,* Forum 4-5, ed. Laura Coltelli.

Permission has been granted to reprint excerpts from *Havasupai Songs* by Leanne Hinton, courtesy of Gunter Narr Verlag; "Two Worlds" from *Mud Woman* by Nora Naranjo-Morse, courtesy of the University of Arizona Press; "Intimate" from *Earthquake Weather* by Janice Gould, courtesy of the University of Arizona Press; and *She Had Some Horses* by Joy Harjo, courtesy of the author and Thunder's Mouth Press.

⊛ This book is printed on acid-free, archival-quality paper.

Manufactured in the United States of America

03 02 01 00 99 98   6   5   4   3   2   1

Library of Congress Cataloging-in-Publication Data
Donovan, Kathleen M., 1946–
Feminist readings of Native American literature : coming to voice
/ Kathleen M. Donovan.
p.   cm.
Includes bibliographical references and index.
ISBN 0-8165-1632-4 (alk. paper). —
ISBN 0-8165-1633-2 (pbk. : alk. paper)
1. American literature — Indian authors — History and criticism. 2. Feminism and literature — United States — History — 20th century. 3. Indians of North America in literature. 4. Indian women in literature. 5. Women and literature — United States — History — 20th century. 6. Group identity in literature. 7. Culture conflict in literature. 8. Race in literature. 9. Oral tradition — North America — History and criticism. 10. Canadian literature — Indian authors — History and criticism. I. Title.
PS153.152D66   1998   97-21197
810.9'897'082 — dc21   CIP

British Library Cataloguing-in-Publication Data
A catalog record for this book is available from the British Library.
Publication of this book is made possible in part by the proceeds of a permanent endowment created with the assistance of a Challenge Grant from the National Endowment for the Humanities, a federal agency.

*To my mother, Lillian Carey McNerney, for teaching me that
the life of the mind is the life that endures.*

CONTENTS

ACKNOWLEDGMENTS

Many people and institutions provided invaluable help while I was completing this book. At the University of Arizona, Larry Evers, Barbara Babcock, and Susan Hardy Aiken gave generously of their time and insights, while the Women's Studies Program and the Summer Dissertation Support Fund provided crucial financial assistance. At South Dakota State University, my colleagues and students in the English department have been consistently encouraging, and I have benefitted from research money provided by the SDSU College of Arts and Science Summer Research Fund as well as the Graduate School's Faculty Research Fund. The Special Collections librarians at the University of Washington in Seattle and Washington State University in Pullman were enormously helpful. My friends and colleagues Joni Adamson Clarke, Nina Bjornsson, Renae Bredin, Toby Langen, and Alanna Kathleen Brown all offered judicious editing suggestions. My children, Karen and Mike, give me continuous support. Finally, my beloved Magic spent many patient hours lying under the computer table, keeping my feet warm during a frigid Dakota winter.

FEMINIST READINGS OF
NATIVE AMERICAN LITERATURE

INTRODUCTION

THE TRICKERY OF FORMS

We think we are limited,
but forms are tricky things.
At the level where hearts dissolve,
maps have no meaning.
We only know ourselves by embracing
what is other, only know the other
by refusing all refusals.
                              —Janice Gould,
                     "*Intimate,*" Earthquake Weather

A few years ago, in a graduate seminar in Native American literary aesthetics, a rising young Native American author/ scholar expounded on his literary endeavors to an enthralled audience of graduate students and professors. The audience of thirty or so was a mixed one, mixed by race, gender, nationality, and scholarly interests. The charismatic speaker was generous and enthusiastic and made a great impression, especially as he discussed his life and his fiction. Following the custom of the seminar, two days after the guest writer's appearance, the group met again, sans writer, to discuss the sessions. As the class progressed, it became evident that the writer had served as a catalyst for bringing to the surface serious and divisive issues that had been percolating just beneath the surface but which, in an attempt to maintain the harmony and sheer joyfulness of the class, no one had been willing to openly address.

While the class universally applauded the writer's fiction and autobiographical work, it divided over his scholarly work, particularly an essay that was very critical of the historical interactions of white women with his people. Some white feminists in the room took exception to his rather sweeping condemnations of white women, pointing out that while white women had indeed been instruments of oppression of Native peoples, they had also been constructed as Other, had also been subjected to the tyranny of patriarchal paradigms, and had learned to speak the master's language and to employ the master's oppressing and colonizing tools as a means of survival. Many students took exception to the white feminists, construing their criticisms as a personal attack on a popular writer and arguing that the feminists in the room looked at everything through a myopic feminist filter. The class came to a standstill when a Native American woman emotionally tried to explain how it felt for her life to be the object of study. "You people," she said haltingly, "talk so easily about literary 'texts' and you theorize so easily about these so-called texts, but you forget, these are our *lives.*" With that, she broke down in tears, and the class session ended in disarray.

When the class convened at its next meeting, it was obvious that the dynamics were forever changed. Despite the best efforts of the professors to heal the deep schisms, the lines were clearly drawn. Class members no longer felt free to express themselves as openly as they had before for fear of hurting another's feelings or bringing criticism down on themselves. No one wanted to be insensitive, and in the desire to restore the previous harmony, however fragile it had been, much was left unsaid. As a result, instead of a dialogue that might have led to mutual understanding, voices were silent, tensions festered, and friendships were broken. People reverted to the invulnerability of pre-set molds of belief and behavior. The trickery of forms held sway.

I have thought of that class many times in the past few years and wondered what we could have done differently. I lost a friendship in that class that I regret to this day. When my friend, a woman of color, and I, a white woman, tried to discuss our feelings about what had transpired, I was amazed at how we talked *at* each other, repeating a formulaic dialogue that neither of us had invented. I had naively believed that we had created a friendship that transcended racial boundaries, so I was amazed to find myself lumped into a category of anonymous feminist "whiteness." My friend felt that I was a representation of a system that had displaced and exploited her land and her people. There didn't seem to be much more we could say to each other without inflicting more hurt and creating more distrust, so we were silent. Once again, the trickery of forms won out.

Today I regret that we did not try harder. I believe that we had much to say to one another and that ultimately our positions were not so different. We accepted the impermeability of forms when in actuality, as Janice Gould's poem says, "forms are tricky things" that can and should be permeated with respect and affection and knowledge. Numerous parallels exist between Native American literature and feminist literary and cultural theories. Native American literature illumines feminisms, and feminisms help us to understand many of the issues raised by Native writers, especially Native women writers. This book was born out of that belief and hope that a dialogue can develop between feminists and Native Americans.

The relevance of even the term "feminisms" to Native American communities is debatable among women. Many white feminist literary theorists have omitted discussion of Native American women from their work for fear of being accused of appropriation. Many conscientious feminist theorists are afraid that "speaking about" constitutes "speaking for," and so simply do not speak at all in matters relating to Native women and their writing. The attitude of some Native women writers toward the word "feminism" is also clouded by individual experience and cultural expectations. For example, Navajo poet Luci Tapahonso does not wish to be identified as a feminist because her tribal culture does not even recognize the word. Another poet, Creek writer Joy Harjo, says that even though the word does not carry over to her culture, a concept mirroring feminism does. Laguna writer Leslie Marmon Silko states that even though she came to feminism differently because of her culture, she is, indeed, a feminist.

Perhaps the most fundamental issue raised by both Native American literature, particularly that by women, and feminist theories is the issue of voice: Who can speak? and how? and under what circumstances? What can be said? And after the ideas find voice, what action can be taken? These questions also underscore the interactive, dialogic nature of writing and speaking because they take critical heed of the audience, the receptor of the message. Women have always talked to each other, bell hooks points out; the necessity now is to find out how and what women communicate across cultural, class, sexual, national, and gendered borders. All of these factors influence the process hooks terms the "revolutionary gesture" of "coming to voice." As she states in *Talking Back*,

> . . . the idea of finding one's voice or having a voice assumes a primacy in talk, discourse, writing, and action. As metaphor for self-transformation, it has been especially relevant for groups of women who have previously never had a public voice, women who are speaking and writing for the first time, including many women of color. Feminist focus on finding a voice may seem clichéd at times, especially when the insistence is that women share a common speech or that all women have something meaningful to say at all times. However, for women within oppressed groups who have contained so many feelings—despair, rage, anguish—who do not speak, as poet Audre Lorde writes, "for fear our words will not be heard nor welcomed," coming to voice is an act of resistance. Speaking becomes both a way to engage in active self-transformation and a rite of passage where one moves from being object to being subject. Only as subjects can we speak. As objects, we remain voiceless—our beings defined and interpreted by others. (12)

This process of active self-transformation belies the popular impression of women of color as passive victims of overwhelming oppression. Women, regardless of ethnicity, find ways to resist. Resistance takes may forms, as these chapters demonstrate. Sometimes that resistance is overt, other times more subtle. Sometimes resistance is heroic; Joy Harjo's poetry, for example, serves as *testimonio* to women activists such as Anna Mae Aquash and Jacqueline Peters, both of whom died violently for their conviction that social justice is not an abstract ideology but a transformational, pragmatic politic. Sometimes resistance is the will to survive against poverty and prejudice, as Maria Campbell's and Beatrice Culleton's autobiographical work demonstrates. Sometimes resistance subverts existing patriarchal social structures without openly attacking them, as the oral poetry of Havasupai women demonstrates. Always, the forms of resistance identified in this study demonstrate that the political is highly personal and that a woman's "coming to voice" is intricately bound up with her culture as well as with her gender.

The movement from object of discourse to speaking subject encompasses several issues that the book explores: 1) the negotiation of identity by those who must act in more than one culture; 2) the agency of women of color interacting with the dominant culture; 3) the feminist reader encountering misogyny in a "canonical" Native American text; 4) ethnographic misinterpretation of tribal women's lives; 5) intertextuality among women's texts from different cultures; and 6) transformation and healing through the rejection of opposition as a cultural value.

Despite the recent explosion of publication in both fields, very little has been written to date exploring in depth the links between Native American literature and feminist theories. Paula Gunn Allen's *The Sacred Hoop: Recovering the Feminine in American Indian Traditions* (1986) pioneered the field and provided valuable discussion of individual writers' relationships to the oral tradition. Allen's work calls for a radical reconstruction of cultural stories, by placing less emphasis on the individual, less emphasis on narrative conflict, and providing more contextualization to achieve what is ultimately the goal of both Native American and feminist ontology—harmony and balance. For Allen, it is through oral traditions that such a radical reconstitution of storytelling occurs, because it provides new ways of knowing through a dialogic potency that is accretive rather than linear, that acknowledges the existence of a sense of time that is achronological, and that places an emphasis on continuance rather than extinction.

In recent years, however, Allen has been criticized for the perceived essentialism in her ideas and for her broad insistence on the gynarchial nature of American Indian tribal structure. This book picks up on several themes begun by Allen and continues the discussion in the frame of dialogue with recent studies in feminist literary and cultural theories, and the related fields of ethnography, ethnopoetics, eco-feminism, and post-colonialism.

The first chapter explores issues related to how Canadian women of mixed blood (Metis) ancestry achieve voice through writing their stories in autobiographies and autobiographical novels. Crucial to finding a voice is the reconciliation of multiple identities inherent in persons who belong to more than one culture. Because they are excluded from both Euro-Canadian and Canadian Native cultures, they negotiate an identity that draws on the strengths of each one. Yet as is evident in the autobiographies of Maria Campbell and Lee Maracle, the first achievement of voice for women of color is sometimes a mediated voice. This chapter also begins an exploration of the role that language plays in the formation of self and tribal identity for Metis women, discussing the work of Campbell, Maracle, and Beatrice Culleton.

The second chapter reminds us that Western privileging of written texts deflects attention away from a potent form of creativity still practiced in most Native communities—the oral tradition, a form to which, historically, women of most cultures were limited, and which was also used subversively by women to alter the restrictive circumstances of their lives. For example, despite ethnographic interpretation of the apparent limitations imposed on Havasupai women, they have always made use of a potent instrument of cultural and self-expression—their songs—which demonstrate that a coming to voice may occur in forms other than writing. As Ruth Finnegan points out, poetry can be a "medium for the normally unsayable" (227). This statement is especially true of oral poetry because of the reciprocal interrelationship of performance, performer, audience, text, and social context. In their songs, Havasupai women created a dialectic that allowed them to be the architects of their lives without tearing down the existing cultural paradigm. Four texts of women's songs dating from the early twentieth century, a transitional time in Havasupai culture, exhibit a remarkable degree of independent thought within a culturally sanctioned forum relating to curing, marital conditions, and female bodily sovereignty, demonstrating the ironic and subversive coding women employ in their artistic expression.

Chapter 3 discusses the work of N. Scott Momaday, who since the publication of his Pulitzer Prize–winning novel *House Made of Dawn,* and continuing with the 1990 publication of his most recent novel, *The Ancient Child,* has been regarded as one of the most generative, representative, and recognizable writers of the "Native American Renaissance." His reverence for the spoken and written word is unmistakable, yet for a writer to whom language is essence, Momaday's representation of women characters raises disturbing issues. To a feminist reader, Momaday's novels are linked by an underlying misogyny that is inconsistent with his philosophy of language and with the search for harmony and balance characteristic of Native American literature. Momaday depicts contemporary women as negative forces whose duplicitous language, sexuality, transgressiveness, and witchery actively subvert the male protagonists' spiritual healing. In his novels, Momaday himself subverts the traditional tribal concept of healing inherent in female fertility by using pregnancy and maternity to silence his disorderly female characters. Using a frame of feminist reader-response theory in conjunction with the theoretical work of Luce Irigaray and Hélène Cixous, chapter 3 explores the paradox of Momaday's phallocratic conceptualization of women's roles with the undeniable attraction of his words.

From the contemporary work of Momaday, the discussion moves to early Native American fiction. Believed to be one of the first Native American women to write a novel, Mourning Dove (Christine Quintasket), an Okanogon woman from north-central Washington, published *Cogewea: The Half-Blood* in 1927, after twelve years of delay and with the help of her editor, the Euro-American businessman and Indian rights activist Lucullus Virgil McWhorter. In his editorial capacity, McWhorter made significant contributions to the novel's revisions. Critics today generally concede that Mourning Dove's voice in *Cogewea* is compromised by the frequency and insistence of the voice of McWhorter, who is credited with the chapter headings and epigraphs, and with the insertion of ethnographic detail and political commentary. To McWhorter, the male Euro-American, is attributed the "authoritative" elements of literary allusion and historical, scientific, and political knowledge, while the less "authoritative" elements of the romance genre and storytelling are attributed to the Native woman. Yet *Cogewea* was a pivotal work in the development of Native American literature, breaking many of the rules for literature by and about Indians. Mourning Dove was a literary subversive and structural innovator, and her influence is evident in the work of today's Native writers. In this fourth chapter, by examining the Mourning Dove–McWhorter correspondence (archived at the Washington State University Library) and another manuscript (archived at the University of Washington) that became the basis of Jay Miller's *Mourning Dove: A Salishan Autobiography,* I intend to show that Mourning Dove was a player in the editorial decisions that produced her novel, that to suggest otherwise implies that a woman of color cannot maintain her agency in dealings with the dominant culture, and that *Cogewea* is an ambitious, collaborative literary work that grew out of a complex relationship between a Native American woman and a Euro-American man.

In response to the traditional tendency of the dominant culture to regard people of color as a monolithic Other, a whole body of critical literature has developed denying the monolothism of minority cultures and the dominant culture as well. Critics now emphasize the specificity of culture and warn of the inaccuracies that arise from drawing inferences about one culture from data derived from another. For women of color, this insistence on specificity helps to establish their cultural and gendered identity. Yet the question must be raised: Is there such a thing as commonality of aesthetic and cultural expression? If we look for such commonalities, are we then complicit in cultural obliteration? On the other hand, if we valorize specificity, do we run the risk of further dividing women from seeking solutions to problems they face across the world? Chapter 5 discusses how two women of color explore these issues in their fiction through their representation of femaleness in their respective cultures. Paula Gunn Allen, a Laguna/Sioux mixed-blood writer, describes her complex novel *The Woman Who Owned the Shadows* as a confluence, a road, a vision quest, and a musical composition. These same metaphors describe Toni Morrison's equally complex work, especially *Sula, Beloved,* and *Jazz.* A close examination of the novels reveals many parallels in the writers' representations of the ways in which, for women, the crucial search for individual and cultural voice is shaped by the Native American and African American oral traditions, and by the relationship of landscape to human action. Such conjunctions in the thought of two writers of color from vastly different cultures and landscapes suggest that cultural specificity need not exclude some very real cultural commonalities.

The final chapter explores the complex link between darkness and femaleness, the romance of the shadow, which is at the heart of the work of Hélène Cixous and Joy Harjo. Both writers deal with the question of how to reconcile their internal need for subjectivity with external historical processes of division without creating dualities, hierarchies, oppositions, and polarities. As Allen points out in *The Sacred Hoop,* Harjo has arrived at her view of the permeability of boundaries from the work of American feminists, but strong congruences exist as well between Harjo's thought and the work of the French feminist Cixous. These congruences are so marked that the two writers almost appear to be engaged in an ongoing dialogue that reveals the transformative power of language to change fear and hatred, the shadowy areas of their lives, into love, by questioning and ultimately rejecting the polarities implicit in phallocentric culture and its discourse.

Connecting all of these chapters is a concern for language, and the ways in which language shapes culture and identity. As the work of James Clifford, Edward Said, Gayatri Spivak, and Homi K. Bhabha have made clear, in the contemporary metropolitan world, both culture and identity are hybrids, and neither is static. In Said's words, "Throughout the exchange between Europeans and their 'others' that began systematically half a millennium ago, the one idea that has scarcely varied is that there is an 'us' and a 'them,' each quite settled, clear, unassailably self-evident" (*Culture and Imperialism* xxv). Because of the necessary hybridity of both culture and identity, the language that expresses them is also necessarily hybrid. Despite the intensive language preservation efforts currently underway in numerous communities, many Native people today do not speak their tribal language, including some of the writers discussed here. Some of them address the difficulty of trying to express tribal concepts in the language of the colonizer. Silko has expressed her anger at the loss of her fluency in Keres. Harjo speaks of the "artificiality" and the "materialism" of English. Metis writer Maria Campbell has adopted what she calls a "village English" that is more natural to her than standard English.

These writers face an additional challenge as women writing in a masculinist discourse; that is one reason why the congruences between the thought and writing of Cixous and Harjo are so marked, as both writers play with language and form, seeking a new way to express a woman-identified resistance to imperialism and dominance. As Said writes, "Gone are the binary oppositions dear to the nationalist and imperialist enterprise. Instead we begin to sense that old authority cannot simply be replaced by new authority, but that new alignments made across borders, types, nations, and essences are rapidly coming into view" (*Culture and Imperialism* xxiv); as the work of all of these creative women demonstrates, these new alignments are already being voiced across gendered and national borders, through the medium of storytelling, whether oral or written, which is, after all, the heart of resistance and continuance.

All of these writers demonstrate the necessity of leaving behind the trickery of forms. When we challenge the forms, as both Native American literature and feminist theory do, we find that we are the ones who created the myth of their dominance and so tricked ourselves into believing in their invincibility. We grew silent, fearful of giving offense or being offended. At the close of the twentieth century, we need to reopen the dialogue, reminding ourselves that "we only know ourselves by embracing / what is other."

1

METIS WOMEN WRITERS

The Politics of Language and Identity

"Damn, Indian women,
especially Pueblo women,
don't drink Pina Coladas
on Kauai beaches
in December and enjoy it!"
— Nora Naranjo-Morse,
"Two Worlds," Mud Woman

Nora Naranjo-Morse's poem "Two Worlds" speaks to the incongruity between the dominant culture's expectations of Native women and the multidimensional reality of their contemporary lives. More importantly, the poem speaks to the internalization of conflicting roles experienced by Native women and asks, "Where was my place in these opposing worlds?" (48).

Native women have been the subject of relentless ethnographic study; some of these studies have provided valuable insights into the lives of their subjects, but much misinformation has been drawn from scholarship flawed by the methodology and biases of the collector. Such misinformation usually resulted in portraits of Native women that continued the stereotype of romantic savages in the wilderness or, conversely, of lowly members of the tribal hierarchy, but certainly did not describe someone who could be found tanning herself on a Hawaiian beach. Even literary works have by and large concentrated on Indian males and the destructive forces of alcoholism, poverty, and suicide on reservations.

Only in recent years have writers given voice to the problems facing non-reservation, urban Indians. Again, many of these works have focused on a male protagonist who leaves home, not always of his own accord, and who suffers multiple assaults on his sense of self before returning to his home and finding a healing of his wounds in his return to tradition. These are the stories William Bevis terms "homing in" novels. As Bevis says, "In Native American novels, coming home, staying put, contracting, even what we call 'regressing' to a place, a past where one has been before, is not only the primary story, it is a primary mode of knowledge and a primary good" (582). The hero, a romantic broken figure of defeat, finds a reconciliation with his roots through the intercession of a tribal elder and the healing power of myth and landscape.

For contemporary urban Indian women, however, the healing is more complex and difficult to achieve. Although they face many of the same problems as their male counterparts—alcoholism, drug abuse, unemployment, poverty, suicide, loss of tradition and iden- tity—they also face problems that are distinctively female-gendered: a loss of power and esteem in formerly matrilineal cultures; the trauma of psychological, physical, and sexual abuse from Native and non-Native men; prostitution; a frequent inability to care for their children, with the subsequent loss of their families to a paternalistic social-welfare system; a high rate of teen-age pregnancy and infant mortality; and, sometimes, an unmistakable, yet usually unexpressed, anger at the perceived passivity of Native men.

Despite these many disadvantages to being an urban, female Indian, there exists at least a sense of solidarity in their Indian-ness, a sense of ethnic and tribal identity that is a major source of strength in facing the difficult realities of their lives. They may be rejected by Eurocentric culture, but they are Indians, free to regard people of European ancestry as outcasts of Native culture. Power and centricity reside in knowing exactly who you are. This sense of solidarity and centricity, which are mitigating strengths to the harshness of contem- porary urban Indian life, is more difficult to achieve for women of mixed-blood ancestry. Neither Indian nor white, they are frequently scorned by both cultures, so the road to identity and healing is more perilous. This is especially true of Metis (Canadian mixed-blood) women who must negotiate their identity and community among multiple, shifting, and sometimes contradictory entities.

In recent years, Metis women have told their stories with unflinching realism, clarity, and even humor by adopting the language and literary forms of their colonizers. This chapter examines several of these recent works: Beatrice Culleton's autobiographical novel *In Search of April Raintree,* and two autobiographies, Maria Campbell's *Halfbreed* and Lee Maracle's *Bobbi Lee, Indian Rebel: Struggles of a Native Canadian Woman.* While their subjects' circumstances differ, and their tones range from personal to political to militant, all of these storytellers see the acceptance, and even privileging, of an Indian identity as crucial to beginning the process of healing.

As the colonized of the colonized, Native Canadians have found their problems compounded by that country's historically complex system of classification for Native people, a legal taxonomy of increasing differentiation, which itself is an instrument of imperialism. The legal definition of "Indian" has changed through time and for varying political purposes. Initially, the term "Indian" was applied by whites to people who lived a non-European way of life. With the miscegenation begun by the fur traders, a melding of lifestyles made such a simple distinction impossible. For a time, "Indian" and "Metis" were legal classifications. Lineage was traced through the mother prior to the 1941 census, so if the mother was classified Indian, the children were also Indian. In 1941, the legal ethnic origin became the father's classification for non-reserve Indians; for reserve Indians, the lineage of both parents was taken into account (Frideres 1–4). As a function of Canada's long-standing "Divide and Conquer" policy, the 1951 Indian Act classified indigenous peoples into several groups who would compete against each other for recognition and benefits. Such tactics had far-reaching implications for Native women.

When she married a non-status man, an Indian woman born with status lost it, unable to regain it even if she subsequently was divorced or widowed. Along with her status, the woman lost her band membership and with it, her property, inheritance, residency, burial, medical, educational and voting rights on the reserve. In direct contrast, an Indian man bestowed his status on his white wife and their children, and could bestow it by adoption upon any other children. Consequently, every Indian woman was dependent on a man—first her father and then her husband—for her identity, rights and status under the Indian Act. (Tobique Women's Group 12)

Such divisionary tactics exacerbated tensions between Native men and women, and between the varying classifications of Natives, particularly between the full-blooded Indians and the Metis. Although the Indian Act was amended in 1985 to eliminate sexual discrimination against Indian women by permitting the bands to determine membership, the problems of the Metis continue. In reality, the 1985 amendment simply shifted the burden of fighting sexist discrimination from the national to the local level, since each band is now solely responsible for determining enrollment criteria.

Central to a resolution of Metis problems is the definition of "Metis," a problem the Canadian government and the Metis have long struggled to settle. Originally consisting of those people with French and Indian (usually Cree) blood, but now consisting of anyone with some Indian blood, the Metis were a legally recognized group until 1940. After 1940 and until the passage of the Canada Act, the Metis were not a legal entity in the eyes of the federal government. Historically, Metis regarded themselves as the people in-between, a part of Euro-Canadian and Native culture, yet belonging to neither.

Twentieth-century Metis leader Stan Daniels described the Metis as people "caught in the vacuum of two cultures with neither fully accepting [them]" (qtd. in Harrison 15). Contemporary Metis insist they are a separate and distinct ethnic group with their own language, history, and cultural identity. Their origins were Native and European, but they do not belong to either group. In the past, the Metis viewed this exclusion negatively, but Metis of the last twenty years insist that this separateness is a strength. They scored a major victory toward official recognition of their special status in the passage of the Canada Act, which specifically recognizes the "existing aboriginal and treaty rights" of Native people, and amends the definition of aboriginal to "Indian, Inuit, and Metis." Just what existing aboriginal rights should consist of is a source of continuing controversy, and many Metis still live in extreme poverty, but the specific naming of them as aboriginals in the Canada Act restores some measure of identity and legal protection.

The influence of more than three centuries of Metis history on contemporary writings by Metis women is powerful and informing. Several historical/social points are especially pertinent to an examination of the texts by Culleton, Campbell, and Maracle.

First, the Metis originated in the fur trade, and the free, nomadic lifestyle was essential to maintaining their culture. Since they did not easily adapt to a different mode of living, government attempts at acculturation through agriculture or relocation were unsuccessful. Metis, like other indigenous people, found urban life demeaning, isolating, and unnatural. Urban Metis are particularly vulnerable to the loss of identity that contributes to a high incidence of poverty, alcoholism, violence, and suicide. Freedom from government control and the right to self-determination are paramount to the Metis self-image.

Second, Canada has long maintained a "Divide and Conquer" policy towards Native peoples that helps ensure a lack of unity among them. The divisions are based on gender and ethnic factors. Historically, Indian prejudice against the Metis was based on the fact that Ottawa pitted its constituencies against each other in competition for land, benefits, money, and recognition. White prejudice against the Metis was based on race, class, and gender. These divisions have been supported not only by official policy and unofficial practice, but also by Christian religions, which have been a demoralizing force in Metis consciousness through the early practice of encouraging a shift to an agriculturally based economy over a hunting and gathering one.

For Native and Metis women, the misogyny of Christianity, with its emphasis on original sin and the evil of female sexuality, held special implications, as did the Jesuit emphasis on patriarchal power. Somer

Brodribb cites the diary of one Jesuit, Paul LeJeune, on the power of women in Native society as he tells a Native man: "in France women do not rule their husbands" (88). Christian marriages also did not permit divorce, as did Native unions. The Jesuits even imprisoned women who left their husbands, with varying degrees of resistance: "On one occasion a woman was kept for twenty-four hours without fire or a blanket, and with scarcely any food. On another a woman who fled from her husband was threatened with being chained by the foot for four days and nights without food" (Brodribb 88). As Eleanor Leacock points out, "the Jesuits, seeking to restructure Native society along hierarchal, patriarchal lines, attacked female autonomy and communal decision-making. The Jesuits correctly saw Native acceptance of White ideology as essential in reordering relations of production and facilitating colonial domination" (8).

In her extensive study of Native American women and the Great Lakes missions from 1630 to 1900, Carol Devens delineates the divisive effects of Christianity and Western culture on the intricate web of gender relationships in Native communities during the early years of the fur trade. In most Native communities, men's and women's activities were separate but complementary. Men's activities revolved around the more solitary pursuits of fishing, hunting, and trapping, while women's activities included communal fishing and trapping of small game near camp, and the harvesting of berries, nuts, and wild rice. Men were in charge of hunting large game animals, but women were in charge of the processing and distribution of the meat, thus giving a woman "her autonomy and her authority to control food while reinforcing a sense of community and interdependence among households" (Devens 12). Women also maintained their own shamanistic rituals, separate from those of men. As a result of interaction with European culture, the carefully attended balance of power began to shift to males, as colonization was not only a legal and religious upheaval, but a social and economic one as well.

Devens describes the "symbiotic" relationship of religion to economics in New France that revolved around concepts of property and production. In their traditional culture, Indians accumulated only enough food and hides to support community needs. But European emphasis on property and accumulated wealth soon disrupted their economic system as the French rewarded settled, Christianized Indians with material goods, cleared land for cultivation, and mercantile privileges equal to the privileges accorded to the French (Devens 15). The Europeans valued the furs obtained by the men as a medium of exchange, especially for food, much more than the material culture of the women. Devens documents the dramatic shift, within a ten-year time span of 1616–1626, in the goods Indians sought for their furs: in 1616, the most sought after goods were food, tobacco, and metal work; by 1626, the most desirable goods were clothing and food, the traditional products of women's work (16). Devens notes that "as women's relationship to the disposal of hides and furs changes, the significance of their direct contribution to the community welfare diminished. As for men, while they too experienced a degree of alienation from the fruit of their labor, their contribution now became the focal one within the economy" (17).

As the economic function of women's work shifted from production to assistance in the preparation of hides, their role in food preparation and distribution also shifted due to increased reliance on European foodstuffs. In addition, economic reliance on furs required frequent moves to new camps, further diminishing women's authority and community.

The Jesuits came to believe that the only truly effective means of conversion to Christianity lay in encouraging the Indians to settle near missions and trading centers. Initially, the missionaries directed their conversion activities towards the men. Believing in the European notion of the male as head of the household, the priests assumed that if the men converted, the women would follow as a matter of course. They were unprepared for the depth of resistance they encountered among many Indian women. To be sure, some Indian women did convert out of genuine belief in Christianity, but many others converted under duress. Some of the converted women found Catholic mysticism consistent with their pre-contact autonomy; Devens documents a cult of the Virgin that developed in some native communities by the 1670s. More typically, however, Indian women clung to their traditional beliefs and rituals, to the dismay of the priests and, frequently, Native men, who, Devens argues, found their mode of living under Christianity to be attractively sedentary. The Jesuits also found the women's attitudes towards marriage and sexuality scandalous, believing it imperative that women surrender their sexual autonomy to men according to European rules of sexual conduct. Native women perceived the threat to their status in their communities and resisted, sometimes violently. The missionaries responded by pressuring Native men to assert their dominance through threats and physical violence, thus setting into motion serious gender conflicts that continue to this day.

The third point that must be considered is that rejection of the Metis by Native and Euro-Canadian peoples resulted in a long-standing confusion over identity that has only recently begun to be restored by the Metis' insistence on, and pride in, a separate ethnic identity. As a result of this double-edged rejection, omission and misrepresentation are characteristic of discussions of Metis contributions to Canadian culture, resulting in a lack of identity among Metis and a continuation of ethnic bias by Euro-Canadians. Such attitudes reinforce the prevalent but erroneous belief among Euro-Canadians that "Canada's true national character results from the superimposition of white European culture on a passive landscape which has no contribution of its own to make" (Morisset 197). In reality, Canada's history is more a process of interaction in what Mary Louise Pratt refers to as a "contact zone," involving the co-existence of people of divergent cultures in the same physical space (*Imperial Eyes* 7). Just as revisionist historians of the United States, such as Patricia Nelson Limerick and Richard White, insist that U.S. history involves much more interaction than the east to west imposition of European culture on a steadily receding "frontier," so also Pratt stresses the nature of the intercultural contact as interactive and improvisational, and far more complex than the simple hierarchal concepts conveyed by words such as "conquest" and "domination." Instead, Pratt's perspective emphasizes "copresence, interaction, interlocking understandings and practices, often within radically asymmetrical relations of power" (7).

Finally, the Metis have a long history of producing strong women, going back to the fur-trade society in which women's contributions were both expected and essential. Sylvia Van Kirk argues that far from being passive victims of the colonialist enterprise, Native women maintained a degree of agency in their dealings with the dominant, patriarchal culture. Contrary to the Eurocentric reports of early ethnographers, which traditionally viewed the ethnographic encounter through the gaze of the colonizer only, the colonized also returned the gaze, resourcefully adapting the most useful elements of the dominant culture.

This process of "transculturation" is characteristic of contact zones. Pratt notes that while "subjugated peoples cannot readily control what emanates from the dominant culture, they do determine to varying extents what they absorb into their own, and what they use it for" (6). The rejection of the view of Native women as passive victims does not deny, however, the reality of their exploitation; instead, it focuses attention on their methods of resistance and subversion (Etienne and Leacock 21). As time passed, succeeding generations of mixed-blood women experienced increased racism and pressure to assimilate. These Metis women maintained intense family ties from a frequently dependent and precarious social position and demonstrated great love for their own mixed-blood children. In recent times, the enforced separation of families by an arrogant social-welfare system has been extremely destructive to Metis identity.

Given the prominence of women in Metis society, it is only natural that literary texts by Metis women feature strong female characters who resist and subvert domination to effect personal and political change. The earliest literary works in English by mixed-blood women—Emily Pauline Johnson's collection of stories *The Moccasin Maker* (1913), set in Ontario, and Mourning Dove's novel *Cogewea* (1927), set in Montana—carry on a tradition and point the way to contemporary writers by portraying women who are caught between conflicting cultures as a part of each while belonging to neither, yet who identify more with Native aspects of their lives to achieve a fused identity that respects both elements.

Johnson and Mourning Dove also used themes and structures that are important in contemporary Metis women's literature: the difficulty in achieving a sense of self-identity and self-esteem in the individual caught between two cultures; the coming to terms with one's mixed-blood status and viewing it as a positive rather than a negative force; the importance of family ties and a unity with nature to any kind of self-acceptance; a warning of the dangers to mixed-blood women in relationships with white men; the hypocrisy of organized Christianity, which preaches universal love while systematically engaging in racist and sexist activities; the importance of a female elder in passing on stories and tradition to younger women; a melding of oral tradition with the written word; and, finally, using both the language and the literary forms of the colonizer to resist and create.

Beatrice Culleton's autobiographical novel *In Search of April Raintree* incorporates all of these themes and structures in relating the story of two Metis sisters who are taken away from their alcoholic parents by the social-welfare system, made wards of the state, and placed separately in various foster homes until the age of eighteen. The novel bleakly portrays the effects of destroying strong Metis family ties, a loss that makes the sisters' search for identity even more problematic. Drawing on the strong Metis oral tradition, the story is narrated in the first-person recollection of the elder sister, April, who at the age of eight functioned as the caregiver for her younger sister, Cheryl, when their parents were too drunk to care for them. Through April's eyes, the loving and tragic urban Metis life is revealed as the novel constantly seeks to balance the positive and negative forces of Metis life.

Culleton, who has taken back her family name of Mosionier, wrote the novel after both of her sisters committed suicide. Since her parents were alcoholics, she and her siblings were raised in white foster homes, so the novel parallels her own experience of feeling little connection to her Native identity for most of her early life. She began writing as a way to find answers to her family's problems.

> As I wrote, it wasn't going to be about a search for identity. But while I was writing that's what I realized about myself: that I had to accept my identity, not to make everything right or things like that. It doesn't happen like that! But it gives me, I think, a strong foundation. I'm not

so wounded by what's happening with Indian problems, and I can get more involved in it by understanding more of their side of the situation, as well as the white side of the situation. (qtd. in Lutz 98)

April, the light-skinned sister, is most like Culleton herself, initially determined to assimilate into white culture. April remembers the love the family shared when her parents were sober, and witnesses the transformation they undergo when drinking. The drinking binges occur just after the welfare checks are distributed, and she sees the demoralizing effect of welfare on her proud father. The Metis tradition of visiting other families for dancing and singing has deteriorated into drunken brawls. During one such gathering, April walks into her parents' bedroom to find her mother in bed with another man. She sees the poverty, dirt, and malnourishment of the other children and feels only revulsion. She identifies with the white children she sees in the park, "especially the girls with blond hair and blue eyes. They seemed so clean and fresh, and reminded me of flowers I had seen" (*April Raintree,* 15). But she is not accepted by the white children, getting her first taste of rejection based on race and class. When social workers come to remove her and Cheryl from their home after the death of their infant sister, she cannot understand the passivity of her parents, who offer no resistance. "My mother should have fought with her life to keep us with her. Instead she handed us over" (17).

Through her years in a foster home where she is a badly treated servant, April learns that being white is an advantage in life. Since she possesses a light skin tone, and because she is naturally repulsed by the alcoholic Native people she sees on the streets of Winnipeg, she tries to emulate a Euro-Canadian lifestyle by reading fashion and design magazines to prepare herself for the time when she intuitively knows she will be wealthy. She marries a wealthy white man and lives with him and his mother on their Toronto estate. Because of her skin coloring, no one other than her husband and his mother knows of her Native blood until her darker sister Cheryl visits and she is confronted with the ethnocentrism of Euro-Canadians:

"Oh, I've read about Indians. Beautiful people they
are. But you're not exactly Indians are you? What is the
proper word for people like you?" one asked.

"Women," Cheryl replied instantly.

"No, no, I mean nationality?"

"Oh, I'm sorry. We're Canadians," Cheryl smiled
sweetly. (116)

When April overhears a conversation between her husband's
mother and his mistress, she realizes he married her to spite his
mother, who does not want to be "grandmother to a bunch of little
half-breeds" (126). April is thus confronted with long-standing elements of Native/Euro-Canadian relations: white men have historically
used Native women for their own selfish purposes, and the prejudice
against Native people is perpetuated by white women in class- and
gender-based competition for the same men. Both Native and non-
Native women are victims of a patriarchal system that commodifies
women and determines their value relative to men.

April summons the self-respect to divorce her husband, but still
convinced of the superiority of Euro-Canadian culture, she ensures a
large monetary settlement to underwrite her lifestyle. She returns to
Winnipeg so that she and Cheryl can live together, but the divisions
between the sisters grow even wider as Cheryl pursues her Native
identity while April is firmly entrenched in her bias against Native
people.

Cheryl is the tragic instrument that brings April to an acceptance
and pride in her heritage. Raised for a time in a Metis foster home,
she educated herself in the history and traditions of the Metis. Cheryl
fills the role of an elder by sending April letters, stories, and speeches
on significant events and leaders, especially the doomed Louis Riel, a
symbol of the Metis fight for autonomy. As a child, Cheryl is a fighter
for her people, willing to undergo punishment at school for correct-
ing Canadian history texts' erroneous and patronizing portrayal of
Metis and Native life. It is Cheryl who goads April from her passivity
and complacency by taking her to a Friendship Centre in Winnipeg to
talk with Native people for the first time in her adult life. Even though

both sisters undertake a search for their lost parents, only Cheryl cares enough about family ties to persevere until she locates their father.

One of the novel's great strengths is the delicate balance it achieves in depicting April's gradual acceptance of her Metis identity in counterpoint to Cheryl's growing disillusionment. Too young to remember their parents accurately, Cheryl has idealized and romanticized them in much the same way she idealized and romanticized Metis history. When she finally locates their father, she learns the truth of the alcoholism that destroyed the family and led to her mother's suicide, and is filled with revulsion. "All my dreams to rebuild the spirit of a once proud nation are destroyed in this instant. I study the pitiful creature in front of me. My father! A gutter-creature!" (217–18).

As her father continually needs money, he drives Cheryl into prostitution and her own developing alcoholism. She begins to see her people through April's eyes and sinks into despair.

> Sometimes I can't help it, I feel like April does, I despise these people, these gutter-creatures. They are losers. But there is a reason they are the way they are. Everything they once had has been taken from them. And the white bureaucracy has helped create this image of parasitic natives. But sometimes I do wonder if these people don't accept defeat too easily, like a dog with his tail between his legs, on his back, his throat forever exposed. (215–16)

After Cheryl is beaten by a customer, April is mistakenly kidnapped, beaten, and raped by three men in another prostitute's search for revenge; Cheryl's disillusionment complete, she identifies with all of the negative aspects of Metis life. "I walk along Main Street. This is where I belong. With the other gutter-creatures. I'm my father's daughter" (225). Finally, she commits suicide in the same manner as her mother, jumping off the same bridge, but she leaves a son whom she named after her father as a symbol of a new beginning. April accepts her identity as she accepts her sister's child, pledging that "for Henry Lee and me, there would be a tomorrow. And it would be better. I would strive for it. For my sister and her son. For my parents. For my people" (228).

Culleton's novel reveals the harshness of life for urban Metis cut off from family ties and nature, forced to live in poverty, dependent on welfare, and fulfilling the stereotype of Native people held by the dominant culture. They come to hate themselves and assume an attitude of defeatism. In classic "homing in" novels, such as Momaday's *House Made of Dawn* and Silko's *Ceremony,* the protagonist achieves a sense of identity by returning home to be healed by tradition, myth, and the land. But the density of city life puts urban Metis out of touch with nature, and their home may be a slum or nonexistent. When Culleton's characters search for their parents in the only neighborhood they can remember, they are disgusted by the squalor.

Culleton's novel underscores the necessity of community in the formation of Metis identity, and the difficulty that contemporary urban Metis women encounter when they search for a community. The Friendship Centres are one possibility, but the novel suggests that new parameters of community may be necessary. Homi K. Bhabha argues that the post-colonial constitution of the modern metropolis demands, with its influx of minority and immigrant groups who seek not so much assimilation as authority and autonomy, such a reconstitution (in Mariani 63). While Bhabha refers specifically to the relationship of Third- to First-World concepts of community, indigenous populations who have been subjected to relocation and displacement experience the same need to redefine their sense of community in relation to their contemporary urban environment. April Raintree's new community may begin with only herself and her sister's child, but it is a community, and it is a beginning. Further, the novel suggests that in its storytelling, stylistically like an oral performance, the continuance of the community is assured.

Even Metis who have a more pastoral environment to return to find that the passage of time has drastically altered their perceptions of community. The reality is that many Metis do not have a place to call home. Maria Campbell, in her autobiography *Halfbreed,* writes movingly of going "home," only to discover it no longer exists: "Going home after so long a time, I thought that I might find again the happiness and beauty I had known as a child. But as I walked down the rough dirt road, poked through the broken old buildings and thought back over the years, I realized that I could never find that here. Like me, the land had changed, my people were gone, and if I was to know peace I would have to search within myself" (7-8).

Among the people who are gone are her mother, her brothers and sisters, and her Cheechum (grandmother), the most influential person in her life, who taught her traditional Metis ways of dress, mores, and culture. Cheechum is also the storyteller of the community, who passes on the oral tradition. In doing so, she impresses on Maria the need to feel pride in her heritage and warns against the "Divide and Conquer" policy of Euro-Canadians: "They try to make you hate your people" (42). Cheechum reinforces the need for the Metis to organize and fight for their personal and political rights, but she also sees that their efforts are doomed by the divisions within their own ranks. For example, when a movie is shown depicting legendary Metis leaders Louis Riel and Gabriel Dumont as buffoons, only Cheechum walks out, while other Metis laugh at the debasement of their history.

Halfbreed continues the indictment of Christianity in its depiction of the priest who shows up for Sunday dinner and eats all the food himself, steals from the Sun Dance pole, and refuses a funeral mass for Maria's mother, a Catholic so devout she never misses mass and puts the family's last money in the collection plate. Even today, Campbell speaks bitterly of the role Christianity played in the colonization of her people: "certainly the church has always been the 'man coming in front of' the oppressor, the colonizer" (qtd. in Lutz 47). The danger she sees now from the church is its incorporation of Native rituals into its own ceremonies as the priests perform ceremonies and go to sweat lodges: "But that's the history of Christianity. When you can't completely oppress a people, if you are losing them, then you incorporate their spiritual beliefs. And that's even uglier than the other way, because then people think 'Oh well, now it's okay, because the priest is now doing our ceremonies.' So the priest ends up being the shaman in the community. And then we have a whole other battle to take on" (qtd. in Lutz 47).

When Campbell's mother dies, the family's situation becomes desperate; eventually the social-welfare system moves in and separates the children by placing them in various foster homes. Her father's way of life, based on hunting and trapping, is becoming archaic. The establishment of a national park on traditional Metis hunting grounds makes him a poacher who is continually sought by the law. Eventually he is forced to take up farming, for which he is totally unsuited. Like April Raintree, Campbell sees the demoralizing effects of welfare on her father, and the increasing alcoholism and violence in her Metis neighbors.

The alienation of the Metis from the dominant *and* the minority cultures runs deep. From childhood they recognize that they are accepted by neither Indians nor whites. Of the estrangement from the Indian world, Campbell recalls,

> There was never much love lost between Indians and Halfbreeds. They were completely different from us— quiet when we were noisy, dignified even at dances and get-togethers. Indians were very passive—they would get angry at things done to them but would never fight back, whereas Halfbreeds were quick-tempered—quick to fight but quick to forgive and forget . . . We all went to the Indians' Sundances and special gatherings, but somehow we never fitted in. We were always the poor relatives, the *awp-pee-tow-koosons* [half people]. They laughed and scorned us. They had land and security; we had nothing. (*Halfbreed* 26)

From childhood, as well, they learn rejection from Euro-Canadians who break up Metis camps, keep Metis under surveillance while they shop, and ridicule their mode of living, including their food. Campbell remembers the shame she felt over the Metis children's school lunches:

> Lunch hours were really rough when we started school because we had not realized, until then, the difference in our diets. They had white or brown bread, boiled eggs, apples, cakes, cookies, and jars of milk. We were lucky to have these even at Christmas. We took bannock for lunch, spread with lard and filled with wild meat, and if there

was no meat we had cold potatoes and salt and pepper, or else whole roasted gophers with sage dressing. . . . The first few days the whites were speechless when they saw Alex's children with gophers and the rest of us trading a sandwich, a leg, or dressing. They would tease and call, "Gophers, gophers, Road Allowance people eat gophers." We fought back of course but we were terribly hurt and above all ashamed. (46–47)

From a very young age, Metis learn they are rejected and ridiculed by two cultures. Their shame turns into self-hatred and reaches serious, destructive proportions in adulthood. Campbell recounts her experiences as an alcoholic, a drug addict, a drug courier for a white man, and a prostitute. Her increasing involvement in Metis political and social causes rescues her, but the "Divide and Conquer" policy is at work within Metis organizations where women have learned to despise the weakness and passivity of Metis men, and the men think the only function women should serve in the organization is secretarial and/or sexual. Further gender divisions wrack the movement. Campbell realizes that numerous social-services programs exist for men, but relatively few for women, even though "society didn't deal as harshly with men on the streets as it did with women" (151).

Campbell recognizes as well that the problems of Native Canadians cannot be solved simply by placing Natives in charge of programs designed to help Native people, because "Whenever they hired Natives to work with Native people, it ended in disaster, with our people being hurt. I remembered how our people were divided and fought each other once their leaders had been hired by the government" (152). Divisions between Indians and Metis continue to hinder a united approach. A proposal to form a federation of Indian and Metis failed because treaty-status Indians feared loss of their treaty rights. "The Halfbreeds," they said, "have nothing to lose, so they can afford to be militant" (155).

While Campbell believes that a political solution is the only way to resolve the problems facing Metis and Indian people, she has been forced to scale back her expectations. "I realize that an armed revolution of Native people will never come about; even if such a thing were possible what would we achieve? We would only end up oppressing someone else" (156). Nevertheless, she sees change coming in a form consistent with a pragmatic utopian vision: "I believe that one day, very soon, people will set aside their differences and come together as one. Maybe not because we love one another, but because we will need each other to survive" (156–57).

Like Culleton's novel, Campbell's autobiography displays the strong influence of oral tradition. Told in the first person, the story transcends the limitations of Western autobiography's emphasis on the individual to encompass a sense of its subject in the context of a community's disruption but continuance. In reality, her book is less an autobiography and more an autoethnography, which Pratt defines as "instances in which colonized subjects undertake to represent themselves in ways that *engage with* the colonizer's own terms" (*Imperial Eyes* 7). A common discursive practice of contact zones, autoethnography uses the language and forms of the conquering culture to provide the subjugated with an entree into the consciousness of the literate culture, thereby gaining the attention of the conqueror and the conquered simultaneously.

Campbell acknowledges the heterogeneity of her audience at the beginning of *Halfbreed* when she considers the purpose and impact her story will have. She recounts how a white friend said, "Maria, make it a happy book. It couldn't have been so bad. We know we are guilty so don't be too harsh" (13). Yet Campbell's purpose is to tell the reality, to multiple audiences, of "what it is like to be a Halfbreed woman in our country" (8). One of her most damning indictments of the colonial process is contained in her statement that "My parents and I never shared any aspirations for a future. I never saw my father talk back to a white man unless he was drunk. I never saw him or any of our men walk with their heads held high before white people" (13–14). Clearly, one of the purposes of the book is to hold Euro-Canadians accountable for their actions.

Another purpose, equally clear, is to relate in a manner accessible to all audiences—Euro-Canadian, Native, and Metis—the composite nature of Canadian history and to stress the necessity of ethnic pride in order to have a future. Recurring throughout the book is the image of "the blanket" as a multivalenced metaphor—warm, protective, a sometimes useful camouflage, but ultimately confining, restrictive, and oppressive. Campbell's Cheechum teaches her that "when the government gives you something, they take all that you have in return —your pride, your dignity, all the things that make you a living soul. When they are sure they have everything, they give you a blanket to cover your shame" (137). Campbell's most convincing assertion of individual and communal identity occurs in the last line of the book, when she declares, "I no longer need my blanket to survive" (157).

For Campbell, the continuance of the oral tradition is one of the principal means of ensuring the survival of the individual and the community. Like Beatrice Culleton, she believes that storytelling is a healing but problematic agent. She defines a storyteller as "a community healer and teacher" (qtd. in Lutz 42) but acknowledges that the literary preservation of stories is a source of continuing intergenerational and linguistic debate. Many of the elders (most of whom are nonliterate as a result of government policy between the Riel-Dumont-led resistance of 1885 until 1951, which prohibited Metis from attending either white or Native schools) believe that stories are sacred and should only be told orally *by* and *to* bona fide members of the community. Campbell's response stresses her belief that change is inevitable and necessary, and that the quest for an "authentic" culture is misguided and misinformed because culture is always an ongoing process. If the stories are not recorded, she believes, they will be lost. If the stories are lost, so also are the people. She argues that just as the Metis incorporated the horse and beads into their culture through the process of transculturation, so will they also incorporate the recording and writing of their oral culture into a literate one (qtd. in Lutz 56).

A related debate is the question of language: should the stories be told only in Cree or Mitchif, or is English an appropriate and viable transmitter of the culture? In contrast to treaty-status Indians on the reserves, Metis were not forced into government schools that prohibited the use of their own language. As a result, Cree and Mitchif are still widely spoken in Metis communities, but Campbell asserts that because change is inevitable, "the new tools for our young people are writing, painting, dancing, singing in English" (56). She is less concerned with the language of transmission than with supporting Native and Metis writers trying to find their own voice in any language so that children will be able to read of nonstereotyped and credible images of their own people.

Campbell's own struggles with the question of language reflect her belief in the hybridity of cultures. Fluent in both Cree and Mitchif, she is struggling now to find her voice in a language that synthesizes her multiple linguistic origins. She recognizes that writing in Cree or Mitchif would seriously restrict her audience, yet when she writes in standard English, she feels "manipulated" by the artificiality of a language "that lost its Mother a long time ago, and what you have to do is, put the Mother back in the language!" (qtd. in Lutz 49). To Campbell, the Mother is the land, but the way to put the land back into the language eluded her until hearing her father tell a story one night inspired her to write in her own voice, in her own naturally broken English. Of her father's influence, she says,

> My father is very close to the land. If you asked him about Mother Earth he wouldn't know how to answer you, because he doesn't know how to say it. But he lives off the land, he's been a hunter and trapper all his life. He respects the land. He's one of those old people who puts tobacco out before he goes out in the morning, sings his song in the morning. But if I asked my father, "What's our culture?" he'd say, "We don't have one," because he doesn't know what "culture" means. And he wouldn't understand if I tried to explain it to him. . . . I've been deaf to him. All these years he had been telling me stories, but I was expecting something profound. (qtd. in Lutz 49–50)

"Culture," then, is the story, the story is the land, the land is the language of home. Campbell relates that she finds her voice now by returning to the dialect of her childhood; her principal writing language of the past ten years has been "village English" because its beauty and lyricism permit her to "express myself much better. I can also express my community much better than I can in 'good' English.

It's more like oral tradition, and I am able to work as a storyteller with that" (qtd. in Lutz 48).

Campbell suggests that the hybridity of her language is a reflection of the hybridity of her identity as a Metis woman in the cultural hybridity of the contact zone, of taking what is most useful from the colonizer and using it to resist and subvert, by making use of the pre-colonization multilingual ability of Native people that Simon Ortiz has addressed. As Ortiz points out, prior to European contact, Native people "spoke not only their mother tongue but that of sister nations and cultures next to them. In the same sense Native American people speaking French, English, and Spanish after European colonization simply were another addition of other languages" (in Coltelli 105). Of course, Ortiz concedes, the fact that European languages were imposed on indigenous people should not be ignored; nevertheless, such linguistic ability in the face of oppression is a component of survival. Like Campbell, Ortiz views Native writing as a marker of "an acquisition of a language, extending the multilanguage ability-facility of Native American people," a marker that retains its roots in the oral tradition of a people in a "spirit of place" (105). And, like Campbell, Ortiz recognizes that place and identity are inseparable: "English is part of that place in the sense that language is source, and if language is extended to include languages other than your own, then that sense of place would not be so different when expressed in another language. What you are connecting with is still that spiritual source, which is that place from which you stand right now" (105). In the temporal and spiritual dislocation of a people, such as the Metis, language is a touchstone that permits the dislocated to connect with an identity and a community. Campbell and Ortiz suggest that English, despite its introduction as an agent of oppression of Native people, can serve as a touchstone through its capacity as a conduit between the people and the land.

Lee Maracle, the subject of the as-told-to autobiography *Bobbi Lee, Indian Rebel* as well as the author of the more reflective *I Am Woman* and *Sojourner's Truth,* also sees language as a key to identity formation and cultural transmission. "For us language is sacred. Words represent the accumulated knowledge, the progression of thought for any people" (*Bobbi Lee* 7). The defilement of language is inextricably linked to the defilement of the land. Like Campbell and Ortiz, Maracle acknowledges that English is also a language of Native peoples, although historically written English was inaccessible to them. In the residential schools, Native children were forbidden to speak their own language, yet at the same time the vocational curricula of the schools did not emphasize written English. As a result, Native young people were functionally illiterate in two languages. Of her own difficulty in mastering English, Maracle says,

> The difficulty for myself has been mastering a language different from my own without having my own. Most of us learned English from parents who spoke English in translation. Many of our parents had been to residential school and thus did not speak the old language any better than the average five year old speaks English. Without academic instruction and without their own language there were no words to articulate complex thoughts, passions, or ideas. (qtd. in Lee et al. 38)

Learning English, or any language, under such conditions is difficult but not impossible; as Maracle points out, Native people learn English, albeit with a handicap, and English becomes a transmitter of their own culture to each other and a tool as they navigate the fractured margins of their lives. English becomes the medium through which she voices, to her own people, her belief that the solution to Native problems is political, with a class- and gender-based agenda, and it is also the medium through which she teaches Euro-Canadians that it is "the intimate knowledge of the self that could transform this world of unbridled waste and butchery of spirit into a world rich with social and natural conscience" (40). She believes change will occur through class struggle that will free oppressed people from the internal colonization they have experienced from the dominant culture.

Unlike Maria Campbell and the characters in *April Raintree,* Maracle appears to have resolved the identity question. In her own mind and in the perception of Euro-Canadians she is Indian, although her father is white and her mother Metis. She recalls going to the home of a white friend after school and the girl's mother exploding, "Don't you know we don't want Indians here?" (*Bobbi Lee* 32). Even her father refers to her as "squaw." Yet Maracle also realizes she can never be a "traditional" Indian: "I also had trouble with the archtraditionalism that was very strong among politically-minded Indians— and still is. A lot of Indians were simply against technology; they wanted to go back to the woods, back to nature. And they actually planned to go back to the forests and live in the old way. Being an urban Métis, I guess, made this kind of thinking seem way out" (118).

Initially her identity as an Indian is due more to her dark skin and her white father's rejection than to any sense of tribalism. Other than a few references to sayings by her grandfather that she recalls at moments of crisis, she feels little connection to family or place. Indeed, as a result of family violence, poverty, heroin addiction, and prostitution, Maracle experiences a deadening of emotion. "I started feeling completely dehumanized, like a vegetable. I actually stopped acting like a human being—didn't laugh, didn't cry, didn't find things funny or sad" (64). Like other victims of extreme trauma, unless something affected her immediate existence, she was uninterested.

Political involvement brings her out of her passivity, but the narrative demonstrates that Native political consciousness is factionalized by class, gender, race, and ideology. She is also keenly aware of the hypocrisy underlying aspects of any liberation movement because of factionalism and celebrities who use the movement, in her view, for publicity.

Ironically, *Bobbi Lee,* which condemns colonization in all its guises, is itself an example of the sort of literary colonization that Native and women writers have long been subject to. While the narrative voice is definitely Maracle's, the intrusiveness of her editor, Don Barnett, is troubling, recalling Gayatri Spivak's question, "Can the sub-altern speak?" Barnett seems to have approached the project with a distinct elitism. He writes in the introduction that it is important that illiterate "peasants and workers" be given a voice and that they "*be heard* by those of us who comprise imperialism's privileged and literate metropolitan minority. Their recounted lives throw our own into sharp relief, while at the same time they offer us fresh perspectives on the processes of repression and revolution from a unique vantage point: *from below*" (11). This blatantly elitist agenda places emphasis on what colonized people can do *for* the dominant culture. In addition, Maracle most certainly was not illiterate. The narrative reveals that she was widely read in the literature of social revolution and was an articulate and forceful speaker for the rights of Native people. In the prologue to the book's reissue, Maracle notes the dual voices and the conflicts between Barnett and herself: "In the end, the voice that reached the paper was Don's, the information alone was mine" (19). She recalls that Barnett once said of his wife that she was " 'almost an intellectual.' It scared me then into silence" (20). Yet, she says, Barnett also helped her gain command of her own voice, believing in her potential as an activist, "but his idea of political struggle was riddled with arrogance, something I loathed, but knew I too was full of" (19).

Much more satisfying is Maracle's unmediated second book, *I Am Woman,* a spiritual autobiography she describes as a "journey" and a "girl-child's quest for the why of the misery and unfairness of her small world" (x). On this journey, Maracle realizes that political action is only one component of justice for Native peoples. Laws can only do so much, and if Native peoples are to end their victimization, they must undergo a spiritual regeneration in a return to truly Native values. Native peoples have been colonized by having their land, their language, their children, their religion, and their stories removed from them. Only by changing themselves, by returning to their true selves, will Native peoples overcome their repression. "Like miners in a shaft we are weighted down by the tonnage of oppressive dirt that colonialism has heaped on us. Unlike the miners, the dirt is heaped upon us deliberately and no one is terribly interested in removing the load of dirt—including ourselves" (11–12).

Maracle argues that Native women must also remove themselves from caring about the opinions of white feminists, who, she believes, have shown little concern for the needs of women of color.

> The women of the world are re-writing history with their bodies. White women of America are a footnote to it all. I am not in the habit of concerning myself with footnotes. I

am concerned about us though. White women figure too large in our minds. Let us stop chasing them about and challenging their humanity at every turn. Let us begin by talking to each other about ourselves. Let us cleanse the dirty shack that racism left us. Let us deal with our menfolk and the refuse of patiarcy [sic] they borrowed from white men. (182)

Maracle's statement makes clear her belief that the real and most effective revolution will occur in the hearts of Native women. The resolution of all ethnic, class, and gender conflicts in Native/white relations, and in Native/Native relations, depends on the actions of Native women to first heal themselves. That Native women hold the true power, she has no doubt.

For urban Metis women no easy solution exists for their numerous and complex problems. Confronted with the racism, classism, and sexism developed over three centuries of exclusion from Euro-Canadian and Native Canadian societies, they are finding their hope lies not in inclusion but in a new-found identity through exclusion, an identity formed on the margins rather than in the center. Because they are not a part of either culture, they can draw on the strengths inherent in both cultures to form their own ethnic identity. Subverting the tendency of the colonizer to view the colonized in a frozen gaze, Metis women negotiate their identity through the complexities of the contact zone that disallows any fixed referential points, such as "home." When "homing in" to tradition and roots is neither possible nor desirable, they are free to develop new traditions and roots that nevertheless derive from a Native consciousness. This new accent on the positive aspect of historical Metis exclusion from culture signifies a new self-acceptance and self-identity among individual Metis. With the realization of who they are, a healing of individual wounds can take place, and Metis can then begin to address the very compelling social and economic problems they face. The work of contemporary Metis women writers is a realistic rendering of the challenge before the Metis, and a testament to the strength they bring to the task.

2

HAVASUPAI WOMEN'S SONGS

A Poetics of Subversion

Havasupai society is a masculine dominated one, and women are in a relatively inferior position. However, this does not mean that the feminine position is an altogether undesirable one. It means, instead, that the feminine course is a limited one, that women have a rather narrowly prescribed path which they must follow to find fulfillment of basic needs or desires. It does not limit the degree of satisfaction obtainable to them, but only the manner in which they may obtain it.

—*Carma Lee Smithson,*
"The Havasupai Woman"

Poetry is not only dream and vision; it is the skeleton architecture of our lives.

—*Audre Lorde, "Poetry Is Not a Luxury"*

B ased upon a review of the limited ethnographic information about the isolated tribe of Native peoples who inhabit a remote and beautiful canyon of the Colorado River in northwestern Arizona, a reader would naturally infer that traditional Havasupai culture was male dominated in the extreme, with masculine and feminine roles clearly differentiated and regimented. From childhood, so the ethnographic record states, females learned a subservient role by example from female relatives and tribal custom. According to Carma Lee Smithson, the only ethnographer to focus her study on what it means to be female in Havasupai culture, "Girls learn at an early age that theirs is a life of submissiveness, that they may not chart their own course, and that always there will be men closely attached to them to whom they must defer. Women apparently learn this lesson well, and are able to adapt themselves to the various roles set for them, or so their calmer acceptance of disappointment or denial would seem to indicate" (164). According to Smithson, a pattern of submission was so ingrained in them by cultural and familial forces that Havasupai women tended not to openly question the inequities, by comparative Western and Native standards, they endured in matters of work, discipline, ownership of property and economic assets, marriage, divorce, widowhood, patrilineality, and patrilocality.

Yet despite ethnographic interpretations of the apparent limitations of their lives, Havasupai women had, and continue to have, at their disposal a potent instrument of cultural and self-definition—their songs—of which a small body of early songs is extant. As Ruth Finnegan points out, poetry can be a "medium for the normally unsayable" (227). This statement is especially true of oral poetry because of the reciprocal interrelationship of performance, performer, audience, text, and social context. In their songs, Havasupai women created a dialectic that allowed them to be the architects of their lives without tearing down existing cultural structures. Four texts of women's songs dating from the late nineteenth and early twentieth centuries, a transitional time in Havasupai culture, exhibit a remarkable degree of independent thought within a culturally sanctioned forum relating to curing, marital conditions, and female bodily sovereignty, demonstrating the ironic and subversive system of discursive coding women employ in their artistic expression.

All of the song texts and translations are from Leanne Hinton's *Havasupai Songs: A Linguistic Perspective.* Hinton, an ethnomusicologist, made her first trip to Havasupai in 1964 to study tribal musical forms. She warns that separating the verbal text from the musical text is a concept unknown to the composers of these songs. "To a Havasupai—and probably to most musicians in most cultures the world over—separation of music and text is a meaningless exercise. One component cannot exist without the other; they are simply parts of the same thing" (100). Finnegan would add another caveat to the discussion: text cannot be separated from performance; to do so violates a premise of orality that the "skill and personality of the performer, the nature and reaction of the audience, the context, the purpose—these are essential·aspects of the artistry and meaning of an oral poem" (28).

Obviously, then, the ideal way to come to a full appreciation of a song is to experience its performance *in* and *as* a member of the community from which it emerges, but it is also true that songs as "verbal art" (Bauman 7) can and should sustain critical aesthetic attention. Larry Evers and Felipe Molina demonstrate this possibility in *Yaqui Deer Songs / Maso Bwikam,* which acknowledges the distinction between "song sound" and "song talk" (28), yet exemplifies the value of even a restricted-in-scope examination of the artistic integrity and cultural significance of the "song talk." Such restricted critical examinations are routinely applied to written poetry; to suggest that oral literature should in some ways be exempt from the same intensity of critical attention is to perpetuate, in Richard Bauman's words, the old elitist and ethnocentric biases that conceptualize "oral literature as simple, formless, lacking in artistic quality and complexity, the collective expressions of unsophisticated peasants and primitives" (7). This approach to oral texts, according to Finnegan, "implicitly insinuates the assumption that, to put it crudely, 'primitive peoples' have no idea of aesthetics" (331). Such thought derives from the pronouncement of ethnographers who have, according to Trinh T. Minh-ha, told us repeatedly that "primitive mentality belongs to the order of the emotional and affective, and that it is incapable of elaborating concepts" ("Not You, Like You" 372). In Western cultural thought, the emotional and affective have also been the domain of the feminine and, thus, of the devalued. Such ethnographic pronouncements are more revelatory of the cultural biases of the ethnographer than of the intricacies of oral poetry with its many and complex rules. To accord oral texts the level of aesthetic analysis that is brought to written texts is to accord them the respect which is their due as works of art and to pay homage to their creators.

Keeping in mind the fact that the following discussion of women's song texts is by definition a restricted one, I want to examine four songs that reveal how Havasupai women used tribal cultural forms to define themselves as individuals and members of a community while, at the same time, creating a dialectic between their gendered creativity and gendered cultural expectations. The songs are implicitly autobiographical, exemplifying H. David Brumble's broad definition of autobiography as "first-person narrative that seriously purports to describe the narrator's life or episodes in that life" (17) Their episodic quality is consonant with the oral tradition and a Native American consciousness of the self formed in collaboration with the tribal community.

While Western notions of autobiography center on the written narration of the individual's life and his/her consciousness of that life, Native autobiographical forms challenge us to reexamine culture-bound concepts of literacy and individuality. In this reformulation, autobiography may be oral as well as written, visual as well as textual. As Hertha Wong points out, Native self-narration is "an illocutionary act that creates and narrates personal identity," and may be "oral or artistic as well as written" (12). Songs and pictographs are eminent examples of nonliterate autobiographical markers of individual identity existing in relation to a larger community. For example, Judith Vander's study of the songs and musical experiences of five Wind River Shoshone women, what she terms each woman's "songprint," reveals "a song repertoire distinctive to her culture, age, and personality, as unique in its configuration as a fingerprint or footprint" (xi).

While Vander's study focuses on Wind River Shoshone women, her emphasis on the interrelationship of "culture, age, and personality" demonstrates the complexities of the process of forming a self-identity in a Native community, a process that Wong describes as "inclusive," "relational," and "dynamic" to a particular community and a specific landscape (14–15). Likewise, the four Havasupai song texts reveal the tension implicit in integrating an individual with a communal identity.

I. "Miya Homaro, Miya Məsiiyo" (Text 15)

Text 15, "Miya Homaro, Miya Məsiiyo," which Hinton dates to the late nineteenth century, is a personal curing song of the same genre as those sung by a medicine man to cure illness. Central to the Havasupai method of curing is the dreaming process to summon *sumáaga* in the form of one or more *sumáaje. Sumáaga* is "a spirit or power in certain living things and natural phenomena" (Hinton 12), such as springs, rivers, rocks, mountains, wild animals, and sky. Since humans cannot perceive the abstract, *sumáaga* appears to humans in the concrete form of a *sumáaje,* a spirit being who can communicate with humans; i.e., the spirit of an animal or natural phenomena. Through the process of dreaming, *sumáaje* communicate with humans in song so that humans may obtain access to *sumáaga.* A song becomes, as Hinton explains, "an actual expression of the *sumáaje's* presence among human beings. And it is the *sumáaje* himself, by his own intention, who brings about the powerful results of curing illness (or creating it, if the song is sung at the wrong time!), changing the weather, ensuring good crops, and generally affecting the course of natural events" (12).

Havasupai medicine-men songs have almost disappeared along with medicine men, but personal curing songs continue into the present, sung by lay people for a dead medicine man's *sumáaje.* Hinton cites one female informant who sings a personal curing song that her mother dreamed (15), so women, as well as men, could be conduits to the spirit world.

While Hinton and her translator, working from a recording, found the words to Text 15 sometimes difficult to hear and understand, this is their translation:

> Sick in bed,
> very sick
> the good people,
> I joined them.
> I roamed about in there,
> so I believed, but
> it wasn't true.
> The good people,
> sky boys,
> sky girls,
> I joined them,
> I roamed about in there,
> so I believed, but
> it wasn't true.
> The good people,

in a flat place
the boys,
the girls,
I joined them,
I roamed about in there,
so I believed, but
it wasn't true,
it wasn't true,
it wasn't true.

(Hinton 271–72)

Text 15 relates the experience of a Havasupai/Hualapai woman during an illness that probably occurred in the 1890s when the Ghost Dance was popular among the tribes. It reflects Havasupai belief that during periods of unconsciousness, the patient actually dies and moves into the next world; if the patient regains consciousness, he or she may recall the "dead" period. References to sky boys and sky girls are common in Ghost Dance songs (Hinton 270). The translation and meaning of "in a flat place" are unclear, as Hinton had difficulty understanding that part of the song.

The repetitious and ritualistic ending—"so I believed, but / it wasn't true, / it wasn't true, / it wasn't true"—may refer to the fact that the patient wasn't really dead, or it may refer to the historic fact that the Ghost Dance's appeal was short-lived for the Havasupai. Sung in the first person, the song itself is an expression of a woman's power in the process of dreaming and of singing the song, offering the possibility of self-cure undetermined by the power of a medicine man. Havasupai women could not be shamans in a formal sense, but they could serve as a *sumáaje's* instrument of healing. As Helen Jaskoski has pointed out, many Southwest and Plains Indians recognized the power of women singers/healers to effect cures for illnesses stemming from "violation of taboo, spirit intrusion, spirit possession, object intrusion, and witchcraft" (119). Since this song deals with the supernatural—the Ghost Dance and life after death—it seems entirely appropriate that a female singer be the conduit of the *sumáaje's* powers.

Women's self-identification in oral poetry is achieved by the explicit and implicit metanarration of the poem which self-consciously calls attention to the woman singing the song. As Barbara Babcock has pointed out in her essay "The Story in the Story: Metanarration in Folk Narrative," such metanarrative devices, which clue the listener or reader to the interpretive frame of play, performance, or story type, are of "crucial importance in the formation of systems of culture" (71). Babcock distinguishes between explicit and implicit metanarrational devices, defining explicit metanarration as "a comment that deliberately calls attention to the narrative performance as performance and communication" (71). Such a comment may be made through narrative embedding, the enclosure of a story within a story, or through opening and/or closing formulae, or through self-commentary. For example, in Text 15, the embedding of references to "sky boys" and "sky girls" calls the listeners' attention to the Ghost Dance ritual.

Implicit metanarration, on the other hand, includes repetition, parallelism, naming, quoting, onomatopoeia, style changes, pronoun shifts, and tense shifts. All of these devices, by moving our attention from one level of the story to another, direct our attention to the story as story and/or as performance (Babcock, "Story in the Story" 73). By deliberately calling attention to the song as both song and performance, the repetitive ending of Text 15, "it wasn't true," is an example of an implicit metanarrative device. As Babcock notes, repetition forestalls and builds suspense while, at the same time, calling our attention to the "act of presenting" (72) by the singer of the song, in this case a woman whose culture decrees her deference and submission.

The attention to craft and aesthetics is demonstrated in the song's parallel three-fold repetition of key lines, such as "The good people," "I joined them," "I roamed about in there," and "so I believed, but." The function of the parallelism is testament to the artfulness of the composition. Further testament rests in Hinton's notes on the "song sound"—the fact that the vowel harmonies and syllabic stresses of Text 15 are unusual for Havasupai songs (271), suggesting even more complete attention to craft. The woman's acts of composing and singing her composition are an expression of her power as a healer. Her ability to focus attention on herself as composer/singer through metanarration is an affirmation of her personhood independent of male control, but not independent of community influence, befitting a sense of self formed in concert with a social context.

II. "Hank Ward" (Text 17)

On the surface, this song, which probably dates from the early twentieth century, is a simple song about a handsome and proud young man, but seen in its conative function, it becomes a potent instrument of social pressure. In oral poetry, brevity does not signify simplicity but rather "discursive concentration," in Paul Zumthor's phrase, in which "meaning emerges from a nonplace, from an unsaid within the mind of the listener, here and now, and can be modified at each performance" (104). The concentrated lyrics of "Hank Ward" reveal the function of proper names, repetition, and performance context in determining meaning in an oral text.

> Hank Ward,
> Hank Ward,
> Hank Ward,
> Hank Ward.
> Williams,
> Williams,
> Williams,
> to Williams,
> to the store there,
> to the store there,
> that's where he went in,
> that's where he went in.
> He's so proud,
> he's so proud,
> he's so proud,
> he's so proud.
> (he has) a string of bullets,
> a string of bullets,
> (on his) belt,
> on his belt.

(he has) boots,
boots,
he's so proud,
he's so proud.
He's wearing spurs,
he's wearing spurs,
he's so proud,
he's so proud.
Hank Ward,
Hank Ward,
Hank Ward,
Hank Ward.

(Hinton 277–78)

While a young Havasupai woman could not directly approach a man she wished to marry, she could make up a song about him. The song would be taken up by her friends and relatives, so that virtually everywhere he went, the man would hear the song being sung in a teasing manner, creating immense social pressure on him to marry the song's creator. As in Text 15, the constant repetition of the simple lyrics calls attention to the song as performance and reflexively to the singer through alternate phrasing of nasal consonant and vowels, as well as through repetition, parallelism, and the use of proper names such as "Hank Ward" and "Williams." In the medium of song, repetitions and parallelisms invite the listener to participate in the performance. Performance, then, moves the oral text from an individual creative act to a communal one, while still retaining the distinctiveness of the individual.

The use and repetition of the proper names "Hank Ward" and "Williams" are also significant to the meaning of the song. Presumably, "Hank Ward" is the name of the young man whom the singer wishes to marry, so the opening and closing four-line repetition of his name provides balance to the song's structure. At the same time, the act of naming him in the song has the effect of increasing the community pressure on him to marry the young woman through the power of individual and collective performance.

Naming the town of Williams may have literal and metaphoric meaning. Williams, Arizona, is the name of the nearest sizable town to the Havasupai Reservation, so his going "to the store there" is probably not an extraordinary event. However, the use of specific place names is sometimes metaphorically significant in Native American storytelling, as Keith Basso has demonstrated for the Western Apache. Because Native American perception of reality is intimately bound to place, "the location of an event is an integral aspect of the event itself, and therefore identifying the event's location is essential to properly depicting—and effectively picturing—the event's occurrence" (Basso 110). The Western Apache method of "speaking with names" allows the speaker to employ a linguistic shorthand that respects "the imaginative capabilities of other people" (109). To an Apache audience, the use of this culturally significant shorthand displays the narrator as one who is "properly modest, properly polite, and just the way it should be. . . . An effective narrator, they say, takes steps to 'open up thinking,' thereby encouraging his or her listeners to 'travel in their minds' " (110).

Although Basso's study is limited to the Western Apache, it seems likely that their "speaking with names method" applies to other tribes' storytelling as well. Leslie Marmon Silko suggests as much in "Landscape, History, and the Pueblo Imagination" when she says, "Pueblo potters, the creators of petroglyphs and oral narratives, never conceived of removing themselves from the earth and the sky" (84). It is conceivable that by mentioning the town of Williams four times in her song, the composer was employing linguistic shorthand about the larger cultural significance of Williams to an audience that would not only understand her "speaking with names" but expect it of her. It is conceivable as well that the emphasis on Hank Ward's pride and his boots, spurs, and bullets takes on added significance for the audience because of some metaphoric association with Williams. Perhaps there existed in Havasupai society stories of what has befallen other proud young men in Williams; if so, the discursive concentration of the song links singer, subject, place, and audience to a larger cultural significance.

In the oral literatures of Native communities, story and place are integral aspects of the narrative that communicate beyond words and bind the community together. Basso relates a cryptic but meaningful exchange between two Apache women at Cibeque on the Fort Apache Indian Reservation in Arizona. In this conversation, one of the women reports her worry over the health of her brother, and the other comforts her by mentioning an occurrence at a specific place where a "line of white rocks extends upward and out, at this very place" (106). This discursive shorthand of "speaking with names" accomplishes several important things; as Basso explains, it permits the speaker to:

(1) produce a mental image of a particular geographical location; (2) evoke prior texts, such as historical tales and sagas; (3) affirm the value and validity of traditional moral precepts (i.e., ancestral wisdom); (4) display tactful and courteous attention to aspects of both positive and negative face; (5) convey sentiments of charitable concern and personal support; (6) offer practical advice for dealing with personal disturbing circumstances (i.e., apply ancestral wisdom); (7) transform distressing thoughts caused by excessive worry into more agreeable ones marked by optimism and hopefulness; (8) heal wounded spirits. (121)

Because of the functional versatility of place names in Native American discourse, it seems likely that the composer of "Hank Ward" intended her audience to "travel in their minds" and associate the literal depiction of Hank Ward's dress and actions in Williams with some unstated metaphoric allusion that was accessible to the community. By encouraging her audience to creatively employ their imaginations, she exhibits the politeness characteristic of one who does not say too much, while at the same time saying enough to strengthen the bonds of the community. She therefore positions herself as a powerful person whose songs reinforce communal strength. If Havasupai women learned their place at an early age, as Smithson's ethnography reports, the female composer of "Hank Ward" learned as well that the power of song could transform restrictive circumstances and strengthen her position in the community.

III. "The Mother-in-Law Song" (Text 18)

Although actually singing about the treachery of her mother rather than her mother-in-law, in this song a young woman complains about the manner in which her family has insisted on her marriage to a man whose family is believed to be wealthy enough to pay a handsome bride price for her. Hinton's translator, "H," explains the traditional arrangement of marriages among the Havasupai: "in the early days, men folk generally ask the young lady to marry not just any family, but they always name some family that have some things so they can get what they need from that family, have horses, buckskins, clothes, those things, then they have the young lady marry that way" (279). In the complaint of this song, the woman's mother, Red Shoot Woman, and brother have promised that if she marries a particular man, unfortunately named Nits-On-The-Penis-Hair, she will have meat, stock, antelope, an outdoor hearth, deerskins, a Navajo rug, and other valuable items. The gifts, however, are not forthcoming, and the young woman feels duped and cheated.

> Red Shoot Woman
> Red Shoot Woman
> she said this to me:
> "My child,
> if you will get together with him,
> if you will get together with him,
> you will eat meat."
> So she said,
> so she told me,
> and I am waiting.
> And I am waiting.
> My brother,
> my brother,
> stock,
> belongings,
> he told me
> they would give them to me, but
> what they told me is untrue,

what they told me is untrue.
I would have antelope,
that is how they would treat me;
an outdoor hearth
that is how they would treat me
a slingshot.
That is how they would treat me,
they told me this, and then—
they told me this, and then—
Nits-On-The-Penis-Hair
Nits-On-The-Penis-Hair
I married him,
I did, and then
a deer hide,
a good thick one,
a good one,
(to wrap around my) calves
then
(I'd be) a good-looking person,
I'd be like that,
that's how I'd be.
A Navajo rug
with thin (lines),
a red wool one,
with a zig-zag design,
(would) be my shawl,
then
(I'd be) a good-looking person,
I'd be like that.
That's how I'd be, but
what they told me was not true,
what they told me was not true,
what they told me was not true.
A thick deerskin
they'd make me good things.
(I'd have) meat,

they'd make me good things.
All different things,
they'd make me good things
this they told me,
this they told me.

(Hinton 280–82)

The young wife cannot openly accuse her relatives of lying and of failure to make good on their promises, but she can make up a song that immortalizes their duplicity and ridicules her husband. The anger of the singer is unmistakable, but a tirade would not have been effective because it was not culturally acceptable for a Havasupai woman to be aggressive in her expressions, and because, in this social context, song is a more potent discursive mode. A speech is an individual act, but a song, once sung, becomes communal and so perpetuates itself. In seeking redress, the wife's complaints assume greater stature if they become tribal complaints. One isolated, dissatisfied woman may be of little community importance, but if her concerns become the concerns of the larger group, then the chances of a successful resolution to her situation increase.

In addition, through the use of the metanarrational device of quoting and repeating her mother's actual false statements—"My child, / if you will get together with him / if you will get together with him, / you will eat meat"—the singer emphasizes her placement of blame on the two people she holds most responsible for her situation—her mother and brother. When the song is taken up by other members of the community, her mother, brother, and husband are certain to feel the community's rebuke and mockery. The fact that the bride used her composing and performing abilities to precipitate a change in her circumstances demonstrates neither helplessness nor submissiveness; rather, it exemplifies her resourcefulness in using a cultural forum to get what she wants: note the repetition of the line, "And I am waiting" (Hinton 280). Chances are good that when this song is taken up by other women, her husband's family will deliver the bride price rather than endure the community's rebuke. There also appears to be a lesson in this bride's situation that will be noted by the families of other young women when marriages are being arranged, so the song becomes political and social exemplar as well.

IV. "The Girl Who Wants To Marry" (Text 19)

In this strongly conative song text, a young woman resists the pressure of her father and uncle to suppress her sexuality. As in "The Mother-in-Law Song," it would be unthinkable for a woman to openly defy her relatives or to express sexual desire in a speech as frankly as the singer of this song, but the song context has the effect of removing her complaint from ordinary spoken language by elevating it to the more fictional and mythic plane of song. As such, the song text has a strikingly contemporary ring that underscores the falsity of the primitive/civilized, simple/complex binary oppositions that Western audiences tend to impose on oral texts. The composer of this song demonstrates that Havasupai women used a complex aesthetic and political process to effect change.

> My father
> and my uncle,
> those two,
> those two.
> My cunt,
> they can't do anything about it,
> they are (not) able to do it,
> they (had better) listen to me.
> My cunt,
> it seems like they are dying over it!
> It seems like they are dying over it,
> it seems like they are dying over it.

The first part of the song emphasizes the futility and desperation of the father's and uncle's attempts to control her sexual desires and makes them look foolish for trying. In the next several lines, the repetitions become a powerful declaration of identity and will, calling into question the Havasupai cultural ideal of femininity equated with chastity:

This is how I am,
I am what I am,
I am what I am,
I am what I am.
I can't be like this,
I can't just sit around,
I can't just sit around,
I can't just sit around.
A good woman,
a good girl.
Anywhere (in the world),
they can't keep watch on her (forever).
She can't just sit around,
they can't make her just sit around, until
(she uses) a cane to get around.
Until she becomes so old
(that she uses) a cane to get around.
They are (not) able to do it,
they (had better) listen to me, (analysis?)
this is how I am.
I laugh at them heartily.
I am what I am,
I am what I am.

Again, the forcefulness of the repetitions and the open mockery underscore the boldness of her refusal to accept the men's edict and her determination to lead her own life. In the next lines she accuses her father of being a trickster figure because he tells her a story of how a woman should behave, and she reemphasizes her intention to "believe my own way":

My father,
what he said to me is false,
it's just a coyote tale
(that) he's telling me here.
Whatever he does
whatever he says

it won't (change me),
that's how it is.
I am the one.
I don't believe him,
instead,
I believe my own way,
I believe my own way.

In the remainder of the song, the singer takes action against the injustice of her situation by turning her body into a large bird that flies to various points in Havasupai Canyon to spy on her people. No longer willing to be victimized, she controls her destiny by flying and spying until she sees Painted Man, the man *she* wishes to marry:

A bird,
a large one,
my body has turned into one
my body has turned into one.
The high rock walls
this place,
I land on one point after another,
I land on one point after another.
At Wavaho
on the top (of the rock wall),
I sit up there,
I look down.
I look down.
I spy on the people,
they are sitting around down there,
they are sitting around down there.
I think about it there,
I do, but
he is not at all good-looking.
When I see this
I move on.
I go that way
to Wii Gl'iiva

through the cleft (of Wii Gl'iiva)
I go through there,
I go on,
I go on.
At Ha Sogyavo
the top,
I land there,
I land there.
I look down,
I spy on the people,
I see them,
I spy on the people.
Painted Man,
a good-looking man,
he's sitting down there,
he's sitting down there.
There I settle down,
my thoughts go there,
I sit down there,
there I am,
there I am,
there I am,
there I am.

(Hinton 284–88)

The final four-fold repetition of "there I am" becomes a powerfully self-defining statement. Given the vehemence of her protest and the forcefulness of her actions, especially since they are couched in the context of a song, a song that would be taken up by other women, it seems unlikely that her father and her uncle would have persisted in their attempts to control her. Indeed, Hinton's informant told her that the woman was successful in her quest to marry Painted Man, the man she chose over her father's best efforts to control her. Thus, a song achieves what spoken language cannot.

"The Girl Who Wants to Marry" is exemplary of the means by which the complexities of oral poetry permit an exploration of the gender dynamics of Havasupai culture. The lyrics reveal not a sub-missive woman mindlessly obeying the dictates of her male relatives, but rather a woman whose sexuality transforms her into a dan-gerously liminal person who successfully challenges the patriarchal social structure, and does it through a socially sanctioned aesthetic convention. Through a complex system of coding and the safety of the song genre, the singer can covertly express what her culture would have deemed "disturbing or threatening if expressed in more overt forms" (Radner and Lanser 414), such as a speech or direct action. Radner and Lanser define coding to mean "the adoption of a system of signals—words, forms, signifiers of some kind—that pro-tect the creator from the dangerous consequences of directly stating particular messages. Coding occurs in the context of complex audi-ences, in situations where some of the audience may be competent to decode the message, but others—including those who might be dangerous are not. Thus a coded text is by definition complex, and its messages may be complex" (414).

In Text 19, the boldness of the woman's first-person statements is off-set by the explicit and implicit coding. The explicit coding comes in the removal of her complaint from spoken language to the more mythic discursive level of song, thus making her statements less im-mediately threatening to her father and uncle, and perhaps permit-ting her a margin of safety through distancing. Implicit coding occurs in her use of metaphors, place names, and, curiously, the invocation of the authority of other cultures.

The metaphoric images of sexuality underscore the need of males in a patriarchal system to control female sexuality by controlling women's bodies. As Bryan Turner has noted, "the feminine body is the main challenge to continuity of property and power" (qtd. in Babcock, "Taking Liberties" 402). Patriarchy is primarily concerned with two aspects of female sexuality: purity and fertility. By ques-tioning the Havasupai feminine ideal of chastity, the singer attacks a patriarchal principle that "male defined structures represent and con-ceptualize their unity and status through the purity of their women" (Sherry Ortner, qtd. in Babcock, "Taking Liberties" 402).

Fertility is the second aspect of female sexuality with which patriarchy is concerned. In Babcock's discussion of Pueblo pottery, she notes that "baby making and culture making are not only not incompatible, they are inseparable" ("At Home" 378). In an agricultural-based society, sexuality is ultimately about reproduction, so control of sexuality/fertility becomes a primary concern of those in power. Babcock goes on to argue, "Their *potteries* [Babcock's emphasis], like their stories, their rituals, and their kinship system, connect the reproductive aspect of generation with the cultural basis of thought, transmission, and 'in a different voice,' clay sings" ("At Home" 378–79). Songs, like potteries, are agents of cultural creation and transmission. For a Havasupai woman to proclaim her sexual freedom in song undermines the semiotics of cultural representation.

The other major metaphor of the song—the woman's transformation into a large bird that flies around the canyon spying on the people—likewise displaces patriarchal assumptions about the role of women. First, through her own power, the woman becomes a creature that is not earth-bound. Flying is freedom from constraint, permitting the woman to go where she wishes and do as she desires. Transforming herself into a bird allows her the freedom to be a cultural insider and outsider simultaneously. This double-edged vision empowers her literally and figuratively. Her spying permits her to view the actions of her people and find the man *she* wishes to marry. On the level of metaphor, it permits her to leave the restrictions of her culture, ironically through a culturally sanctioned form of representation—the song.

Since the role of place names in oral literature has already been explored in discussing the previous songs, I do not want to dwell on it here, because the same function seems to be at work in this song. The fact that three specific sites in the canyon are named very likely has metaphoric significance to the Havasupai and calls attention to the singer as the performer of the song. In addition, her use of the explicit metanarrational device of referring to coyote tales also self-consciously calls attention to her storytelling gifts. Equating her father with Coyote moves her listeners to an entire corpus of allusions to human foibles, and so strengthens her determination to, as she says, "believe my own way."

One of the most intriguing metaphoric devices she employs in this composition is the appeal to authority to support her claim of independence. Such appeals are a traditional part of telling a story, but the singer of this song puts a new twist on things by appealing not just to intracultural authority, but also to intercultural authority:

A good woman,
a good girl.
Anywhere (in the world),
they can't keep watch on her (forever).
(Hinton 285)

The significance of this intercultural appeal is marked by a shift in pronoun voice from first to third person in this section of the song. When the text resumes its statements of her will and identity, it reverts to first person. The effect of the pronoun shift is to move her complaint from the realm of one woman's experience to create a sense of solidarity with women in other restrictive cultures. Scholars are rightly cautioned against too quickly making inferences about one culture based on data and theory from another, but here we have a situation in which a woman from a so-called "primitive" culture appears to be invoking similarities with women from cultures "anywhere (in the world)."

The final crucial element that marks this song as distinct is the subversive presence of the woman's laughter, which she directs at her father and uncle. The lines, "I laugh at them / heartily," are framed by the lines, "this is how I am" and "I am what I am" (Hinton 285), suggesting that she wishes the relationship of her defiance to her derision to be unmistakable to her audience. Gloria Anzaldúa notes, "When she transforms silence into language, a woman transgresses" ("Haciendo caras" xxii). When the language creates a woman's laughter at male dominance, the transgression is doubled. Of the transgressive nature of women's laughter, Catherine Clement observes the frequency with which female witches laugh in literature and how laughter marks a point of no return from transgression (Cixous and Clement, *The Newly Born Woman* 33). Women who laugh at male dominance live in the interstices of power structures, possessing their own energy and power, which makes them dangerously liminal. Such open laughter at male dominance is clearly transgressive in Havasupai or any culture, yet the singer is able to use it to her advantage within the language of the song.

I believe it significant that all of these songs date from the late nineteenth to the early twentieth century. During this time, enormous pressures were being brought against traditional Havasupai culture from intrusions by the outside, Euro-American world and other Native peoples. Because of their remote and largely inaccessible location in a side canyon of the Colorado River, the Havasupai were protected from many of the intercultural disturbances that other Southwestern tribes faced. They were culturally and linguistically close to their neighbors, the Hualapai, and they made regular trading excursions to the Hopi to the east, but they always retreated in the summer months to the river basin. The first Euro-American explorer to reach the Havasupai, Father Garcés, recorded in his journal in 1776 the fears of his men as they crawled on their hands and knees along the nine-mile trail into the canyon, so steep and narrow was its descent. Isolation was the Havasupai's protection.

But in the late nineteenth century, their protected mode of living came to an end as Anglo ranchers began usurping their water holes, and the federal government claimed the land along the Coconino Plateau, forcing the Havasupai to live year-round in the narrow canyon that could not support their population. The following years brought hardship from epidemics and the forcible removal of their children to government boarding schools. Under such cultural pressures, it seems plausible that a cultural form of expression, the song, would reflect and even actively define the changes that the culture and the women, in particular, were undergoing. As Ruth Finnegan notes, oral and written poetic forms "can be used to influence people's ideas, introduce (or combat) change, uphold *or* challenge the political order—and a whole range of other possibilities" (268).

For the women of a culture for whom poetry already serves as an agency of change, the oral poetry of their songs was both cultural and personal text of subversion. By re-creating their lives in song texts, Havasupai women were empowering themselves within a changing cultural paradigm. Under a phallocentric social system, a woman's attempt at constructing herself as subject is subversive, because once she begins to perceive herself as subject, she can no longer be controlled by phallocentrism. Poetry is one of a woman's vital means to claim the subjectivity that permits her a fusion of her knowledge and feelings. Such fusion arises from, in Audre Lorde's words, the ancient and hidden and dark places within each woman where there exists "an incredible reserve of creativity and power" that leads to knowledge and action (36–37).

In their song expressions of their power or their dissatisfactions, Havasupai women created themselves by reinventing their lives as the subject of song. The fact that they used an acceptable cultural forum makes their re-creations of their lives ironic and subversive. Exemplifying poetry as action, they were seeking a more egalitarian culture for women without openly challenging the existing cultural paradigm, itself already engaged in an intense battle for survival from external forces. The singers of these songs also demonstrate that despite the claim of ethnographers working from a Eurocentric cultural bias, Havasupai women were far from helpless victims; instead, they were cultural architects through their skillful manipulation of language and aesthetic purpose. Refuting anthropologist Evans-Pritchard's claim that "The primitive woman has no choice, and given the duties that go with marriage, is therefore seldom able to take much part in public life" and "She does not desire, in this respect, things to be other than they are" (45), Havasupai women challenged the inequities they faced both publicly and privately, and they did so through a system of complex linguistic and aesthetic coding that allowed them a much wider range of thought and action than was apparent to ethnographers. Their songs, while rooted within a specific cultural context, are representative of the methods of ironic subversion women employ. This subtle method is described by Trinh T. Minh-ha in *Woman, Native, Other:* "Never does one open the discussion by coming right to the heart of the matter. For the heart of the matter is always somewhere else than where it is supposed to be" (1).

3

"A MENACE AMONG THE WORDS"

Women in the Novels of N. Scott Momaday

*Clearly, then, the first act of the feminist critic must be to be-
come a resisting rather than an assenting reader and, by this
refusal to assent, to begin the process of exorcising the male
mind that has been implanted in us.*

—Judith Fetterley,
The Resisting Reader

*"Have gun, will travel" is just as fitting a theme for academic
achievers as it was for Paladin.*

—Jane Tompkins,
West of Everything

*It is how you feel
about the women.*

—Simon Ortiz, *"Apache Love,"* Woven Stone

The generative influence of Scott Momaday in the current
"Native American Renaissance" has been voiced by numerous contemporary Native writers. His is such a looming presence that the very process of undertaking a feminist deconstruction
of his representation of women in his novels feels like a transgression
of the first order. He is a brilliant, lyrical writer whom, on one level,
I want to admire uncritically for the elegant artistry of his use of language. At the heart of his work is his reverence for the spoken and
written word. "In the beginning was the Word," Tosamah intones in
House Made of Dawn; like the Gospel of St. John, Momaday's words
reverberate with all the resonant power of the most finely crafted language. Yet, as Adrienne Rich reminds us, "beautiful language can lie"
and "the oppressor's language sometimes sounds beautiful" (123).

As a feminist reader, my admiration for Momaday's body of work makes my discomfiture with his representation of female characters paradoxical and disturbing. Is it possible to admire a writer for *how* he says something, while disliking *what* he says? This question is especially pertinent with a writer to whom language is essence. In his essay "The Man Made of Words," Momaday articulates the connection between linguistic and experiential reality: "It seems to me that in a certain sense we are all made of words; that our most essential being consists in language. It is the element in which we think and dream and act, in which we live our daily lives. There is no way in which we can exist apart from the morality of a verbal dimension" (162).

In a paradigm where language is essence, form cannot be separate from function. Yet Momaday's two novels, *House Made of Dawn* and *The Ancient Child,* are linked by an underlying misogyny; however beautiful its expression, such misogyny is inconsistent not just with Momaday's philosophy of language but also with the search for harmony and balance characteristic of Native American literature. Yet Momaday's novels consistently represent contemporary women as negative forces. In the novels, Momaday subverts the sacredness of tribal stories, songs, and ritual to the subtly profane purpose of devaluing women. If women are devalued, language, in Momaday's own formulation, is violated. Furthermore, because Navajo ontology underscores the achievement of *hozhon'i* as necessary to any cure, no true healing of the male protagonists can occur, since the creation of such beauty depends on the harmonious balance of male and female. In *House Made of Dawn* and *The Ancient Child,* we are witness to the darker side of the power of language; language endangers even as it creates. As one chapter title of *The Ancient Child* aptly states: "There is a menace among the words" (90).

The problem of misogyny in Momaday's fiction has deeper implications than just the usual grist for the patriarchal mill. After all, as Judith Fetterley points out, "American literature is male" (xii), and Momaday, as a highly educated and well-read man, writes out of an Anglo as well as a Kiowa tradition. The structure of *The Ancient Child* attests to his multiple influences in its intermingling of oral traditions in the Kiowa myth of a Bear Boy with the mythic Anglo folk hero Billy the Kid. That the work of a male writer is misogynist is no great surprise; what troubles me is the fact that his words still have an undeniable attraction that does not permit me to simply lay his books aside as I do with most other writers of similar ideological bent. Furthermore, I am acutely conscious of the fact that in taking Momaday to task for his negative representations of women, I am engaging in the same sort of academic gunslinging that Jane Tompkins regrets in *West of Everything,* when she says, "although it's not the same thing to savage a person's book as it is to kill them with a six-gun, I suspect that the nature of the feelings that motivate both acts is qualitatively the same" (231).

Even though the prospect of engaging myself in the same bloodless violence practiced by phallocratic writers seems counterproductive, Momaday's very stature as a writer demands that his ideas not go unchallenged. In the emerging "canon" of Native American literature, his is a "normative" and "touchstone" voice that, as Barbara Hernstein Smith notes of canonical literature in general, "begins not merely to *survive within* but to *shape and create* the culture in which its value is produced and transmitted and, for that very reason, to perpetuate the conditions of its own flourishing" (50). Nor should I, as a reader, ignore the tension in the paradox of repugnant ideas expressed in eloquent language. Judith Fetterley's 1978 *The Resisting Reader* and recent studies in feminist reader-response criticism by Patrocinio P. Schweickart and Elizabeth A. Flynn are useful for exploring the process of "immasculation of women by men," whereby "as teachers and readers and scholars, women are taught to think as men, to identify with a male point of view, and to accept as normal and legitimate a male system of values, one of whose central principles is misogyny" (Fetterley xx).

Fetterley argues that women are taught to read as men, that the universal viewpoint assumed in culturally authoritative texts is nearly always male, and that women readers must resist the total annihilation of their own experiential authority. Yet, the process of becoming a "resisting reader" is problematic because female readers are always positioning themselves in opposition to male-gendered experience, an exercise in negativity. Even the terms "female readers" and "male readers" assume a universality of experience that does not consider the ramifications of ethnicity, class, and sexual orientation in the encounter between reader and text.

As Schweickart, Jonathan Culler, Diana Fuss, and others have pointed out, reading/interpretation is ultimately about power. Reading is not a passive activity; it is, instead, the locus of intersection between literature and praxis through the reader's interaction with a text (Schweickart 39). In canonical texts, the gendered reader is nearly always male. What are the repercussions to literature and praxis if the gendered reader is one whose experience and perspective have been subsumed under the generic masculine? Schweickart argues that when the reader is male, "the text serves as the meeting ground of the personal and the universal. Whether or not the text approximates the particularities of his own experience, he is invited to validate the equation of maleness with humanity. The male reader feels his affinity with the universal, with the paradigmatic human being, precisely because he is male" (41).

For a male, then, the act of reading is empowering, but the process of immasculation is disempowering to a female reader. Not only does she not find her experience articulated, but the text forces her into the divisive position of reading with a bifurcated vision, as the universality of the internalized male reader struggles against the particularities of the female reader. Such bifurcated vision forces her to read the text in a way that it was not intended to be read; in effect, "reading it against itself" (Schweickart 50). Reading is about power; when women readers have to constantly engage in an act of resistance in order not to be subsumed by a text, they not only cannot expect to find their experiences given a credible voice, but more importantly, they cannot give voice to the very ideas that shape a more egalitarian ordering of the world. What finally disturbs me most in Momaday's representation of women is that in his refusal to even attempt to sympathetically articulate the experiences of his contemporary women characters, he silences them. By silencing his women characters, he silences me. By consistently representing women as negative forces whose perversion of language demands their silencing, he effectively perpetuates the phallogocentrism that feminism seeks to undermine.

Angela Grace St. John, the principal female character of the Pulitzer Prize-winning novel *House Made of Dawn,* enters the narrative as the Angelus is ringing, in a scene juxtaposed with Abel's remembrance of the military tank bearing down upon him. That she will work in opposition to his healing is foreshadowed by Abel's perception of natural phenomena: the sounds of roosters crowing, the morning air "cold and deep," and the "hard and pale" land (27–28). Angela is always associated with disturbances in the natural world and with a sense of separation from nature and ritual. She looks for "some sign of disaster on the wind. Now and then she watched the birds that hied and skittered in the sky, but the birds always went away, and then the sky was empty again and eternal beyond all hope" (34).

Obviously, Angela associates nature with desertion and death. Even her own body and the unborn child she carries repulse her: "She could think of nothing more vile and obscene than the raw flesh and blood of her body, the raveled veins and the gore upon her bones. And now the monstrous fetal form, the blue, blind, great-headed thing growing within and feeding upon her" (36).

Since Angela regards herself paradoxically as alien to nature and also as a loathsome natural representation, the attraction to her physical beauty by Abel and Father Olguin is dangerous, for in her manipulativeness she "knew how to learn at her own expense, and eventually she would make good the least involvement of her pride" (35). After the Feast of Santiago, which we view through Angela's objectively panoramic gaze, she finds a unity with nature as she realizes that she despises Abel for his beating with the rooster by the Albino. As Larry Evers has pointed out, her final impression of the ceremony is sexual ("Words and Place" 305).

As she intended, Angela initiates a sexual relationship with Abel; as she did not foresee, Abel controls the relationship. The narrative does not tell us how this transformation of Angela from dominance to submission comes about, but it suggests that women are rendered helpless and malleable in the face of sexual attraction to a man, and are transformed by making love to him. "She was not herself, her own idea of herself, disseminating and at ease. She had no will to shrug him off" (60).

The scene of Angela and Abel's first lovemaking is juxtaposed with the scene of the Albino stalking Francisco in the cornfield. At the feast, Angela had "keened" to the Albino's unnatural qualities, demonstrating the narrative linking of the evil inherent in them. They are linked, as well, by their white hands in the couplet, "Angela put her white hands to his body / Abel put his hands to her white body," which is immediately followed by Abel's memory of how in death the Albino's white hand looked "open and obscene" (94). Despite her name, Angela functions more like an angel of death.

Angela's transformation into submission works only with Abel; with other men she retains her detached and derisive stance. Ironically, her presence in Walatowa, "By the *grace* [my emphasis] of the last few days," permits Father Olguin to feel "content" for the first time in his surroundings. Such relaxation of his own sense of displacement proves dangerous. When Father Olguin misreads her politeness as interest, he fatuously decides to visit her and take her into his confidence about important priestly/male business while still retaining the protective patriarchal hegemony: "She would *perceive* that he was occupied, committed to a remarkable trust, and she would envy him—not his accomplishments, perhaps, but at least his possibilities. The prospect of her envy pleased him, and he hummed about in the rooms of the rectory until it was noon, and he rang the Angelus long and loud" (66).

Angela, however, has no intention of having her bells rung by the aged priest; in a scene of devastating rejection, she mocks him in the language of his own priestly ritual. " 'Oh my God,' she said laughing. 'I am heartily sorry . . . for having offended Thee.' She laughed. It was hard and brittle, her laughter, but far from desperate, underlain with perfect presence, nearly too controlled" (68).

For Father Olguin, the controlled laughter is more devastating than the rejection, another example of inappropriate laughter by a woman, a prominent feature of the text discussed later in the chapter. Ironically, just as Angela was brought to a reconciliation with nature through the perversion of the *corre de gaio* ritual, so also the priest loses his sense of identity with Walatowa through Angela's perversion of the confessional rite. Returning to the village and seeing the carnivalesque revelry, he focuses on the fly-infested face of an infant and is filled with fear and revulsion as the head turns "slowly from side to side in the agony of sad and helpless laughter" (69).

Our final view of Angela occurs years later at the Los Angeles hospital where a broken Abel is recovering from a severe beating. Angela's entrance and exit in the narrative are bookended by the crowing of the roosters and her talk of her son Peter, whose favorite story is the Indian myth of the boy who turns into a bear. The biblical allusion to roosters and Peter, in a text replete with biblical allusion, seems clear. Angela's sexuality betrays Abel by removing him from the healing possibilities of ritual and landscape.

Angela's role in the narrative and her growth as a character have been problematic for critics. Susan Scarberry-García's sensitive study views Angela as undergoing a positive transformation during the seven-year time span of the novel. "The early scenes portray her as alternately cold and vicious in her designs on Abel. . . . Yet the later scenes portray her as compassionate and understanding." Through her sexual liaison with Abel, she achieves both "pain and knowledge of the natural world. After she returns home to California her power builds accordingly. For, in the hero/heroine pattern, returning home galvanizes power." Finally, Scarberry-García sees Angela transformed from "a person in need of balancing her own life into a protective healer of Abel" (62).

I wish to explore several issues that arise in viewing Angela as a positive force. First, Angela is pregnant when she begins the affair with Abel. In tribal societies, a pregnant woman is generally considered to be an honorable person, but Angela has transgressed boundaries by being an adulterous pregnant woman. As such, her honor becomes problematic. In Mary Douglas's terms, she is "matter out of place" (35), dirt, anomaly, only doubly so. She is literally out of place in Walatowa, due to her race and reason for being there (for the mineral baths to cure a sore back), and figuratively as a woman carrying one man's child but making love with another. By crossing boundaries she is a polluter. Pollution occurs when the "lines of structure, cosmic or social, are clearly defined," as they are in tribal society, and "a polluting person is always in the wrong" (Douglas 112). Such marginal people are dangerous because they permeate societal boundaries. In this configuration, femininity is sexuality is power is danger.

In such an equation, it is unlikely that Angela is concerned with Abel's well-being. While she undoubtedly has feelings for him, she allows two days to elapse from the time Benally notifies her of Abel's injuries until her hospital visit, and Abel seems to sense her danger when he turns his head to the wall as she speaks to him. After arriving for her brief visit, she tells Abel a vague story of "a young Indian brave . . . born of a bear and a maiden" (169), a story that Evers has characterized as "rootless as a Disney cartoon" ("Words and Place" 317). Significantly, it is the rootless Benally who sends for her, Benally who prefers acculturation in Los Angeles to the reservation, where there "would be nothing there, just the empty land and a lot of old people, going no place and dying off" (Momaday, *House Made of Dawn* 145).

Angela's sense of awkward displacement during the hospital visit is palpable. Her words are rushed and rehearsed, Benally tells us, "like she knew just what she wanted to say" (169). In conventional small talk, she says in rapid-fire fashion that Peter was too busy with his friends to visit, and that "she had thought about *him* [Abel] a lot and wondered how he was and what he was doing, you know, and she always thought kindly of him and he would always be her friend" (169). As she makes her hasty exit, she tells Benally "she was awfully glad I had called her, because she wouldn't have missed seeing him again for the world" (170). Since she offers no help to Abel other than the vague storytelling, is she really a positive force that would enable him to see that his only hope of survival lies in returning to Native ritual and landscape? Her ease in using manipulative language, even though it is given voice by an equally glib male character, further casts her as a potent "menace among the words."

The other major female character in *House Made of Dawn,* the social worker Millie, who attempts to acculturate Abel to life in Los Angeles, is likewise dangerous to his healing because of her perversion of the sacredness of language and her sexuality. Millie believes in "tests, questions and answers, words on paper . . . She believed in Honor, Industry, the Second Chance, the Brotherhood of Man, the

American Dream, and him—Abel" (99). Like Angela, Millie is sexually attracted to Abel and sleeps with him, but he sees through her schemes on him and her easy laughter.

Again, the trope of inappropriate laughter is significant. Like Benally, Millie has severed her connection to the landscape of her youth. Her memory of her Oklahoma childhood is filled with the pain of her father trying to break the land but instead being broken by it. The text also connects her to the whiteness of Angela and the Albino in the numerous references to the whiteness of her body. Millie is no less a victim than Abel; however, since Abel's healing can take place only in his own landscape, her attempts to tie him to her through language, acculturation, and sexuality make her as dangerous and manipulative as Angela.

Two minor but significant female characters also figure in the novel's developing misogynistic focus, but their roles have been virtually overlooked by critics. Fat Josie is the sympathetic but grotesque woman Abel turns to after the deaths of his mother and brother, despite Francisco's warnings. Since she has cured him before, Abel goes to her seeking maternal tenderness, in defiance of his grandfather.

> She crossed her eyes and stuck out her tongue and danced around the kitchen on her huge bare feet, snorting and breaking wind like a horse. She carried her enormous breasts in her hands, and they spilled over and bobbed and swung about like water bags, and her great haunches quivered and heaved, straining against her ancient, gray dress, and her broad shining face cracked in a wonderfully stupid, four-teeth-missing grin, and all the while tears were streaming from her eyes. (107)

That Abel receives tenderness and nurturing from Josie is obvious, but why does Momaday characterize the only female who wants nothing from Abel in such grotesquely equine terms? The description of Josie's dancing is juxtaposed with the scene of Abel regaining consciousness on the beach after the beating by Martinez (a scene in which he imagines that "his whole body was shaking violently, tossing and whipping, flopping like a fish" [106]) and his regaining consciousness on the battlefield as the tank bears down on him while he is "giving it the finger and whooping it up and doing a goddam *war dance*" (108). That these three acts of motion—Josie's dancing, Abel's body flopping like a fish, and his war dance—are related by violence and grotesquery is clear, yet Momaday seems to suggest that female tenderness is an element of the violence.

Untangling this complicated weave is no simple matter, but the text offers some clues. First, the significance of Josie's description in equine terms should not be overlooked. Emblems of motion and journey are fundamental in expressing Navajo and Kiowa ontology, and the horse was the principal means of mobility. In addition, horses are associated with self-sacrifice, loyalty, and fertility. In the story of Santiago, his horse tells Santiago to sacrifice him for the good of the people; from the horse's blood, "there issued a great herd of horses, enough for all the Pueblo people" (40).

In Benally's vision of Abel's journey home, the words of the Horse Song are central to an understanding of what Abel seeks: "I am Everlasting and Peaceful. / I stand for my horse" (155). On the horse, Abel could imagine himself at peace. "You felt good out there, like everything was all right and still and cool inside you, and that black horse loping along with the wind. . . . You were coming home like a man, on a black and beautiful horse" (154). In Benally's vision of Abel's vision, a doubly reflective mirror, the horse carries Abel to a healing in the context of the land. "And at first light you went out and knew where you were. And it was the same, the way you remembered it, the way you knew it had to be; and nothing had changed" (154). The horse also carries him to the squaw dance at Cornfields and his assignation with the girl named Pony, whose graceful description stands in counterpoint to Josie's: "There was a girl on the other side, and she was laughing and beautiful, and it was good to look at her. The firelight moved on her skin and she was laughing. The firelight shone on the blue velveteen of her blouse. . . . She was slender and small; she moved a little to the drums, standing in place, and her long skirt swayed at her feet and there were dimes on her moccasins" (156).

But the vision of Pony at the dance at Cornfields is Benally's vision of Abel's vision, and the reality is that Pony becomes, like

Abel's dead mother, just one more memory of a woman who deserts him. What he is left with is the heavy awkwardness of Josie's dancing and her gap-toothed grin in a tear-streaked face; in short, the emblem of the "grotesque realism" of Bakhtin's carnival. Peter Stallybrass and Allon White's discussion of this Bakhtinian concept points out that grotesque realism "uses the material body—flesh conceptualized as corpulent excess to represent cosmic, social, topographical and linguistic elements of the world" to effect "transcodings and displacements" between the body and the exterior world (*Politics and Poetics* 8–9). Momaday has used grotesque realism to effect transcodings and displacements earlier in the novel as he describes Father Olguin's disillusionment with Walatowa, emblemized by the Indian child's fly-infested, corpulent face:

> Its little eyes were overhung with fat, and its cheeks and chins sagged down in front of the tight swaddle at its throat. The hair lay in tight wet rings above the eyes, and all the shapeless flesh of the face dripped with sweat and shone like copper in the sunlight. Flies crawled upon the face and lay thick about the eyes and mouth. The muscles twitched under the fat and the head turned slowly from side to side in the agony of sad and helpless laughter. (69)

The description of the Indian child matches the description of Josie for the grotesquery, mockery, and ultimate tragedy underlying carnival. Bakhtin's grotesque realism "images the human body as multiple, bulging, over- or under-sized, protuberant and incomplete. The openings and orifices of this carnival body are emphasized, not its closure and finish" (Stallybrass and White 9).

Stallybrass and White note the prominence of the carnivalesque as emblem in the literature of colonial and post-colonial cultures, where "the political difference between the dominant and subordinate culture is particularly charged" (11), which is certainly the situation in Euro-American/Native American cultures. Father Olguin struggles to understand the Native souls in his charge. Not until the end of the novel, as Abel informs him of Francisco's death, is he able to say with any certainty, "I understand" (Momaday, *House Made of Dawn* 190).

In Bakhtin, the presence of grotesque realism is a positive sign of vitality. In this paradigm, it is possible to conceive of the Indian child and fat Josie as politically affirmative transgressions of the dominant "high" culture of Eurocentrism by the minority "low" indigenous culture.

What makes the paradigm problematic, at least in the case of Josie, is the fact that she is transgressing both the dominant and the minority cultures (Francisco's warnings to Abel about her). Perhaps it is more accurate to say that she represents—on a personal, as opposed to political, level—the diminished but real choice of female nurturance left to Abel. As he abandons or is abandoned by every other female character, she is the one constant who can cure and nurture him, and who demands nothing in return. Her equine representation, however rudimentary and grotesque, emblemizes the concept of self-sacrifice for the communal good. The horse as emblem of motion permits Josie a positive transcoding, whereas Father Olguin's emblem of motion, his automobile, carries him to a negative transcoding by turning him away from the people.

Momaday's tempering of women's negativity in the problematic portrayal of Josie extends into his treatment of ancestral women such as Tosamah's grandmother, Aho, who is described in a reverential, elegiac passage as a storyteller who "had learned that in words and in language, and there only, she could have whole and consummate being" (88). Aho understands that language is essence and that to corrupt words is to corrupt being. It is important to note, however, that Aho is dead, and Tosamah's remembrance constitutes a lament for the passing of an individual woman and the tradition she represents. On a textual level, it implies the superiority of ancestral women to contemporary women, whose language is duplicitous, perverse, manipulative, even evil.

In Momaday's characterization of the second minor but significant figure, he continues this association in the fleeting mention of Porcingula's sexual relationship with Francisco, which results in the birth of a stillborn child. Porcingula is described as "the child of a witch" and is punished for her high mocking laughter and her sexual perversion in the death of their child at birth. Porcingula's laughter is specifically associated with her transgressive state: "The women of the town talked about her behind her back, but she only laughed; she had her way with their sons, and her eyes blazed and gave them back their scorn" (184). She directs her laughter not only at community mores but at individual men as well. As Francisco calls her name in the grove of cottonwoods by the river, "at last she came out of hiding, laughing and full of the devil. 'Well, you were early after all,' she said, 'and Mariano had not done with me' " (184). As her pregnancy advances, she forsakes laughter, but after the infant's stillbirth "she threw herself away and laughed" (185).

As noted earlier, a preponderance of laughter, especially inappropriate laughter, is associated with female duplicity, sexuality, manipulativeness, witchery, and grotesquery. Laughter's link to evil is suggested by the Albino's "old woman's laugh, thin and weak as water" (77). When Angela scorns Father Olguin, she laughs derisively. Abel is put off by Millie's easy laughter: "Easy laughter was wrong in a woman, dangerous and wrong" (99). Pony's laughter at Cornfields, fat Josie's gap-toothed grin, the Indian child's "sad and helpless laughter," and Nicholás teah-whau's mocking curses emblemize the female transgressive nature. Laughter becomes a perverse female counter-ritual. Catherine Clément comments, "She laughs, and it's frightening—like Medusa's laugh—petrifying and shattering constraint" (Newly Born Woman 32). Noting the frequent laughter of Kundry in Parsifal, Clément points out that women witches often laugh. "All laughter is allied with the monstrous. . . . Laughter breaks up, breaks out, splashes over. . . . It is the moment at which the woman crosses a dangerous line, the cultural demarcation beyond which she will find herself excluded" (33).

In all of the textual incidences of inappropriate laughter, the women are following an innate propensity to disorderliness, Momaday suggests, which makes them dangerous to the status quo. By permeating accepted boundaries established by patriarchal societal custom, in their liminality, they represent danger in their "creative formlessness." Mary Douglas has noted that "the danger which is risked by boundary transgression is power. Those vulnerable margins and those attacking forces which threaten to destroy good order represent the powers inhering in the cosmos. Ritual which can harness these for good is harnessing power indeed" (161).

If ritual is capable of forcing good from disorder, might it not be capable of forcing evil as well? Momaday's text seems to suggest as much. These transgressive women are undoubtedly powerful forces working against the male's well-being. Ancestral women, such as Tosamah's grandmother Aho, derive their benevolent power from ritual and the oral tradition, but Momaday's contemporary female characters either do not know, stand outside of, or have rejected these traditional means to power. Like witches, they live in the interstices of power structures, possessing their own energy and power, which make them dangerous to established (male) power. In Julia Kristeva's definition, they represent abjection, that which disturbs identity, system, order, boundaries, and rules, and "laughing is a way of placing or displacing abjection" (8). Porcingula's loss of laughter during her pregnancy symbolizes a loss of power as she is transformed by Francisco into something "whole and small and given up to him" (Momaday, *House Made of Dawn* 185), but after the child's death-birth, she regains her laughter/power/evil as she rejects Francisco.

In the female characters of *House Made of Dawn,* Momaday depicts women whose duplicitous language, sexuality, transgressiveness, and witchery actively work against the male protagonist's reconciliation with his identity through a return to traditional myth, song, and landscape. They are strong women in a basic, disorderly way, but Momaday betrays their strength by insisting on the primacy of their need of a man and their intrinsic desire for subservience. Likewise, the three female characters of *The Ancient Child* are strong, independent women on a superficial level, but they also have a fundamental impulse to subservience, sexual and otherwise, to a man.

The text goes to great lengths to establish Lola Bourne and Alais Sancerre as financially independent and sexually secure enough to take the initiative with men. Neither woman would ever introduce herself by her husband's name, as Angela does in the earlier novel. But the text confuses the appearance of strength with the reality by suggesting that strong women are those who have careers, manage their own money, and make advances to men, while ignoring the more important quality of not finding their *raison d'être* in serving the needs of men.

The list of characters describes Lola Bourne as a "beautiful, ambitious woman," but her ambition seems entirely for Set, a successful, fashionable painter whose work has become prisoner to his success. The text describes Set as one who had "compromised more than he knew. He had squandered much of his time and talent; he had become sick and tired" (37–38). Set paints in order to "astonish" God, whose boredom with human matters is "infinite. Surely we humans, even with our etiquette, our institutions, our mothers-in-law, ceased to amuse Him many ages ago" (39). Set's malaise is obvious, but why Momaday chooses to gender-inscribe God's boredom is not so obvious unless it is considered in the context of the value his novels place on contemporary women.

Set views women only as objects. He recalls a portrait he sketched of Lola at a picnic on a wind-swept Point Lobos. Set likes the result, but Lola considers it to be not her but "the perfect likeness of a peasant girl named Vivienne, who lived in twelfth-century France, whose father worked for seventeen years on the south tower of Chartres Cathedral, and who was said to understand the language of chickens, ducks, and geese" (54). Set paints Lola as, and she identifies with, a portrait of a female who has no identity in her own right. Like Angela in *House Made of Dawn,* who is associated with the crowing of roosters, the text associates Lola with a woman who understands the language of barnyard fowl. Since the earlier novel develops a hierarchy of animal value based on "tenure in the land" (56), the association of pivotal female characters with lesser animals implies a parallel hierarchism of male and female.

Set's objectification of women continues in the juxtaposition of the picnic scene with his remembrance of the childhood sexual abuse he received from the nun who "liked to loom, bat-like" over him. In the cathedralesque silence of the schoolroom, he hears the sounds of his friends playing outside on the lawn and is "overwhelmed with the sense of banishment." As he withdraws from her after vomiting in her thighs, he notices a "yellow and purple bruise inside and above one of her knees. It resembled an ancient scarab he had once seen in a glass box" (54). The perversion of the scarab's symbolic representation of life, in the anatomical vicinity of the womb as source of life, placed as it is alongside the image of the perversion of mammalian nurturance in the nun's bat-like representation, mirrors the female perversion of religion and sexuality that occurs in Set's encounter with the nun.

The abuse scene is then immediately juxtaposed with a scene in an art class in which the instructor notes the bodily perfection of the female model. "Her body is whole, vital; every bone and muscle and tendon is in place. Her body is soft and yet firm, resilient, round, smooth, delicate, endlessly expressive; and it functions, it serves its purpose" (55).

Set's artistic training enables him to objectify women. Only through art can Set maintain control of women. The bodily perfection of the model permits no disorder, no dirt. Every part is in its appointed place and functions as it should, without challenge, and in discrete entities that are part of the process of objectification, and, ultimately, of silencing. The art studio is, of course, an artificial environment, and the passive, silent perfection of the model cannot be duplicated in real, whole women, who trick, seduce, possess, abuse, and abandon him. Like Abel in *House Made of Dawn*, Set is haunted by a sense of abandonment from the early death of his mother. That Set feels conflicting emotions about women and their bodies is obvious. He cannot forget his revulsion and shame in the incident with the nun, yet he also uses his artistic training to emotionally distance himself by sketching Lola as a twelfth-century peasant girl; by remembering the beetle-like bruise on the nun's leg; by seeing the female body as useful boundaries of the plane which "define your limits" (55); and by emotionally removing himself from his Parisian seduction by Alais by wondering, "who might be observing them in this set piece [an intentional pun?], this rich composition worthy of Gaugin" (208). Clearly, art and the emotional distance it provides are his defense against transgressive women.

Since he naturally objectifies women, Set cannot view women except through the filter of his own desires. Lola comes into his life as the buyer of one of his paintings, the disturbing self-portrait of the dwarf about to be transformed. She becomes his lover at her initiative, but after a time their passion, or more precisely Set's, begins to cool from the demands of his work and the beginnings of his transformation into the Bear. Lola, however, remains a "good sport" (153) who will care for his ailing father while Set goes to Paris for a showing of his paintings at the gallery owned by Alais, and his subsequent affair with Alais.

Like his characterization of Angela in *House Made of Dawn*, Momaday's characterization of Lola is replete with sexual manipulativeness and duplicity. In the body-painting scene, the text specifically connects her to a witch (156). Lola uses her sexuality to control men, creating a heightened tension between Lola and Set, between Lola and Alais, between Lola and Jason (Set's agent), and between Set and Jason. In Set's voice, "She was very pretty in a halter, shorts, and sneakers. I knew that Jason must be very much aware of her presence, agitated by it. He was sexually excited by her, and she knew it and teased him when she pleased" (112).

This passage is revealing on a number of levels. First, it implies that women use their sexuality to control men. Second, it implies that women are unable to control this impulse to manipulate. And third, men are helpless in the face of universal female manipulation. Finally, it suggests a sexual tension between the two males, underscoring Luce Irigaray's contention that in a phallocentric culture women are a commodity for which men compete because woman's value lies in her interchangeability among men (192). The concept of commodity implies the necessity of "at least two men to make an exchange. In order for a product—a woman?—to have value, two men, at least, have to invest (in) her" (181). Patriarchal society depends for its very existence on the exchange of female commodities, Irigaray states, for "without the exploitation of women, what would become of the social order? What modifications would it undergo if women left behind their condition as commodities—subject to being produced, consumed, valorized, circulated, and so on?" (191). The conclusion Irigaray arrives at is that phallocratic culture would function much differently in essential "relation to nature, matter, the body, language, and desire" (191).

Momaday's culture, as evidenced by his novels, is still very much a phallocratic design in which women are always objects, never subjects. In this paradigm, essentialism is the only possible outcome. When the equation of woman = commodity = object is applied to sexuality, the female as object/commodity is self-evident. As commodities, Lola and Alais are interchangeable. The text describes Alais in terms very close to the initial description of Lola's professional pedigree. Both women are independently wealthy, but each works in professions nonthreatening to males. Lola is a librarian and music teacher who also enjoys a respected reputation as a cataloger of fine books, even though we never see her engaged in any work other than promoting Set's talents. She is a perceptive appreciator and collector of art, especially Set's. Alais owns a successful gallery in Paris with a "first-rate" clientele. She, too, has a special appreciation of Set's work. The emphasis on the business acumen and artistic success of the women adds an interesting dimension, as if Set seeks affirmation of his own success and value through valorization by the women. If so, commodities play an expanded utilitarian role as a self-reflexive mirror for the commodifier.

As commodities, women compete sexually with other women, Momaday suggests, in the tension between Lola and Alais, and between Lola and Grey. The tension between Lola and Alais is particularly pernicious as they battle for Set's attention in New York. Lola is cast into the role of "Bitch" because of her unreasonable possessiveness. Instinctively, she and Alais perceive the other as the enemy, having internalized the phallocentric concept of woman as the dark continent, unknowable and always to be feared, especially by herself. In Cixous's words, "they have committed the greatest crime against women: insidiously and violently, they have led them to hate women, to be their own enemies, to mobilize their immense power against themselves, to do the male's dirty work" ("Sorties" 68).

In this paradigm, women who are already an-Other by virtue of their femaleness, conveniently emblemize other women as Other. From a phallocentric perspective, self-effacement is a desirable quality in an-Other/commodity, which explains why all three female characters are willing to assign primacy to Set's needs. For example, Alais serves very little function in the text other than fulfilling Set's sexual fantasies and assisting him in his career. On the day after his show in Paris and their one-night affair, he learns from "good sport" Lola that his father is dying, an event that requires his immediate return to San Francisco. Alais is never mentioned again; having fulfilled the promise of her name, she is simply "a lay."

Lola is equally self-effacing. As Set begins his transformation into the Bear, the power of myth and ritual overcomes her innate possessiveness and jealousy of Grey, and she is able to subdue her "bitchy" qualities for Set's welfare. "Lola Bourne was more than a shade off *balance* [my emphasis]. She looked fleetingly into Grey's eyes and nodded. In some reach of her mind she thought of trying her luck, but in this alien place she had none, and she did not know what to do or say, how to be" (Momaday, *Ancient Child* 255). As Grey touches the medicine bundle in a ritualistic motion, Lola understands that "she had no *purchase* [my emphasis] here, that gratitude is all she could have expected or hoped for" (255). The commodity recognizes in appropriately economic terms that her value must be subjugated to Set's mythic fate, that her role in his transformation is simply to be his chauffeur, and that now another commodity assumes primacy in his story. "The two women held hands without embarrassment, and there was a giving over, a reconciliation, a benediction" (255). In delivering Set to Grey, Lola has served her purpose, which was always secondary to Set's, and she "feels one with herself for the first time in a long while" (255). Lola achieves her own transformation and balance, the text suggests, by valorizing the primacy of Set.

Of the three female characters in *The Ancient Child,* the portrayal of Grey is the most problematic and disturbing because she is the female character most closely aligned with myth. As a visionary and medicine woman, her powers are totally directed to helping Set achieve his destiny as the Bear. "Don't imagine that you have a choice in the matter, in what is going on, and don't imagine that *I* have one. You are *Set;* you are the Bear; you will be the Bear, no matter what" (271). Medicine people in Native culture possess a gift used to benefit the entire community, but Grey's powers are used only for Set. Grey poses the question, "What is it to pass into legend?" (182). For women, passing into legend in Momaday's formulation requires the assumption of a self-effacing, subservient, and ultimately depersonalized role. "It was Set's story that must be told, and no matter how many times the story had been told in the past and would be told in the future, and no matter how crucial was her voice in the present telling, it was he, Set, whose story it was." That "this was simply, profoundly so" (248) is the assured and patronizing stance of the narrative voice.

What Momaday never questions is the assumption that the story of Set as the Bear *must* give priority to the male when the myth involves one boy and his seven sisters. Could not the myth emphasize just as meaningfully the fate of the sisters as the stars in the Big Dipper? Even in the legend of Billy the Kid, which parallels the Bear's story in Grey's visions, women's purpose is solely to serve Billy's needs for sexual pleasure or to assist him in his escapes from the law.

When the paradigm is structured on phallocentrism, it follows logically that the story will emphasize the male, but such a paradigm is itself the result of phallocratic thought in which women are universally devalued. In Cixous's description of literary history, "It all comes back to man—to *his* torment, his desire to be (at) the origin. Back to the father. . . . Subordination of the feminine to the masculine order, which gives the appearance of being the condition for the machinery's functioning" ("Sorties" 65).

The phallocentric paradigm derives from a thought process that, in Trinh T. Minh-ha's words, originated in the "immemorial days when a group of mighty men attributed to itself a central, dominating position vis-à-vis other groups; overvalued its particularities and achievements; adopted a projective attitude toward those it classified among the out-groups; and wrapped itself up in its own thinking, interpreting the out-group through the in-group mode of reasoning while claiming to speak the minds of both the in-group and the out-group" (*Woman, Native, Other* 1).

That a phallocentric system of thought is of such long and powerful standing does not preclude the positing of other systems of thought, nor does alterity imply inferiority. Indeed, the very concept of hierarchy is called into question. In a system of thought built on multiplicity and difference that does not presuppose opposition, when the connection between logocentrism and phallocentrism is finally severed, "all the stories would be there to retell differently" (Cixous, "Sorties" 65). This means that the story of the Bear and his seven sisters could "subvert every notion of completeness and its frame remain a non-totalizable one. The differences it brings about are differences not only in structure, in the play of structures and of surfaces, but also in timbres and in silences" (Trinh 2), and such timbres and silences can only add to the story, not devalue it. When all of the stories are rewritten, history will be altered and the effect will be "incalculable" on the concept and function of society (Cixous, "Sorties" 65).

There can be advantages to men, as well, in the reformulated stories. The fate of the two principal male characters in *The Ancient Child* is not exactly enviable. Grey's question, "What is it to pass into legend?" is as problematic to them as it is to the women. For Billy the Kid, passing into legend requires his early and violent death. For Set, the legend carries him to an existential loneliness, to the death of his human self in his rebirth as the Bear, whose failing human voice cannot be understood by his sisters. In a nonpatriarchal telling, perhaps the legend could be one of healing and reconciliation in a community.

Again, because of Grey's pivotal role in the creation of myth, her devaluation is possibly the most painful to witness. Like Lola and Alais, she is superficially very strong, so strong in fact that she is able to exact her circumcision revenge on her rapist and still ride off on her horse to listen to the voice of the Grandmother, who presumably tells her to look in on Set sleeping in the arbor. Momaday handles the rape scene in an especially insensitive manner that assumes his readers will participate in the insensitivity. From her visionary lovemaking with Billy, Grey is transported into the reality of Dwight Dicks's brutality. The text describes the attack as "horrible and ugly and dehumanizing," yet even as it is happening, Grey must find "the appropriate response" by taking control of the situation and circumcising the rapist. No after-effects of the rape are ever mentioned except the "seed of sorrow, well below the level of articulate indignation, let alone rage, that would now be with her the rest of her life" (97). If Grey feels such sorrow and anger, she hides it well. Indeed, the text shows more concern for Dwight Dicks's pain when the turtle-masked Grey, in a scene of intended comic surrealism, inquires after his injury. How truly comic this scene is depends on the reader's perspective; it is evident that in this scene Momaday envisions the reader as a male who can appreciate the comic horror and puckish presence of mind of Grey's revenge. This male-gendered reader is meant to alternately recoil and feel sated in the punishment.

But to a female reader, Grey's response is not realistic. Not only is the pain of her degradation denied, but the narrative assumes a masculinist stance that the proper response for a woman in this situation is to return violence with violence, and that a woman is capable of plotting her violent response even as she is being violated. Further, it attempts to invalidate the more realistic female response of fear, outrage, and humiliation. The fact that Grey is wearing a turtle mask as she confronts her rapist is also unsettling. In most Pueblo cultures, turtle is a life-bearing creature, similar to the Egyptian scarab, the marking that Set notices on the inner thigh of the nun who seduces him. Does the turtle mask function much like the nun's scarab-like bruise, as a perversion of the female life principle?

The rape scene also is troubling on a number of other levels. Not only does it diminish Grey's fear, pain, and degradation, but it also perpetuates the rape mythology that women fantasize about being raped. It is crucial to remember that when this scene begins, Grey is envisioning making love to Billy, and she is enjoying it. What other conclusion is the reader, male or female, to arrive at?

At the "Poetics and Politics" seminar at the University of Arizona, Momaday defended his inclusion of this scene in the novel. Responding to a European friend's criticism of the rape as an example of American fixation on violence, Momaday said, "I don't have to do that [include sexual violence], but it's true. It's true to . . . the traditions of American literature, this is one of the ways in which we express the equation of the frontier in American history, you know. It's not a pastoral. It's a . . . murder mystery" ("Poetics and Politics" 24).

In this statement, Momaday links the violence of the frontier with sexual violence committed against women. Speaking of the role of the dime novel in shaping American thought about the frontier, he says,

One goes back to the dime novel, I think, and the idea that the Wild West is indispensable to the American imagination. There is no such thing without the Wild West. The wild, you know, it begins somewhere back with the discovery of America, and with Scott Fitzgerald's last paragraph, in which he talks about the green breast of the new world, and Dutch sailors looking west to something commensurate with their power of imagining. And, the dime novel is as I see it a kind of a direct reflection of that fascination. The Boston bank clerk who could go and buy a Ned Buntline novel and take it home and just be transported into a wilderness that satisfied all his cravings . . . and then even more wonderful was the fact that, by God, it was there. People could go out on the Oregon Trail and find Indians . . . in the grass, that's a terrible, exciting feature of America. . . . ("Poetics and Politics" 23)

In this admittedly off-the-cuff passage, Momaday collapses the ideas of wilderness and femaleness into the metaphor that Annette Kolodny examines in *The Lay of the Land,* with the double entendres of the title fully applicable: the "experience of the land as essentially feminine—that is, not simply the land as mother, but the land as woman, the total female principle of gratification" (4). Furthermore, Kolodny points out, just as Momaday does above, "*this* paradise really existed" (5). As Kolodny makes clear, canonical American literature has relentlessly imagined the landscape as female with terrible environmental repercussions—women and mothers are easy to abuse, frequently forgiving, and always possessing further resources to exploit. In *The Ancient Child,* Grey functions as an emblem of violence committed by "civilization" against the land. Her rape is more than the rape of a woman; it is the rape of a mother, of the life source, the land. The land will eventually enact its revenge on its despoilers, just as Grey seeks her revenge on Dwight Dicks. In Julia Kristeva's reading of Leviticus, circumcision symbolizes the separation of the male from the maternal or unclean nature (*Powers of Horror* 99). It seems the ultimate transgressive act and display of power by the defiled (the female) to forcibly effect this separation as an act of revenge. And still, we are left with the remembrance of Grey's pleasure in Billy's lovemaking at the beginning of the rape scene. If Grey is emblematic of the land, as Momaday seems to suggest, is he also suggesting that the American landscape was somehow complicit in its defilement by being too paradisiacal, and so invited its own destruction?

Other inconsistencies in Grey's characterization abound. As a medicine woman, Grey is rather incompetent in giving the medicine bundle to Set before he is ready to appreciate its significance. Set's premature opening of the bundle and examination of its contents unleashes many negative forces. Furthermore, even though Grey is presented as a powerful person, the text trivializes her in descriptions of her personal appearance and her speech. In one lengthy passage, Grey describes herself in the hyperbolic rhetoric of the dime novel: "Is it any wonder that I inspire the praises of Master Bonny? No indeed, for I *am* a bonny lass" (*The Ancient Child* 18). As if to underscore the unreliability and triviality of Grey's self-description, the narrative voice immediately undercuts Grey's voice with a more realistic description. Like one of Momaday's favorite poets, Grey has a propensity for wearing white and even writes Emily Dickinson-like poetry. Her reading tastes are analogous to those of Emma Bovary. Like Emma, Grey is positioned as a "reader of inferior literature — subjective, emotional, passive," while Flaubert, a male, "emerges as writer of genuine, authentic literature — objective, ironic, and in control of his aesthetic means" (Huyssen 189–90).

The inscription of mass culture as feminine reached its height in the nineteenth century, the time of both Flaubert and the dime novel, an age of tremendous social upheaval and challenge to traditional (patriarchal) power structures. As Huyssen points out, many of "the masses knocking at the gate" (191) were women who saw in the combined developing forces of socialism and feminism the possibility of redress for the comparative inequities they endured. The turbulence of the times was reflected in discourse that "consistently and obsessively genders mass culture and the masses as feminine, while high culture, whether traditional or modern, clearly remains the realm of male activities" (Huyssen 191). Literature of the "lower order" is then expressly gender-inscribed as feminine and transgressive. The under-cutting of Grey's voice in such an abrupt manner demonstrates the vast difference between the elegance of Momaday's prose and the exaggeration of the dime-novel prose. Momaday appears eager to assure his audience that despite his professed affection for the dime novel, and although pleasure and escape may be found in reading "pulp," he is firmly in control of his aesthetic and literary purposes.

Grey's language poses other problems. Throughout the narrative, when speaking in her own voice, her language remains casual with many slang expressions, a diction inappropriate to her mythic role. However, when she and Set arrive at her mother's home, we are told that her speech undergoes a profound change. We are *told* this by the narrative voice, but we never hear the change in Grey's own voice. The last words that Grey speaks in her own voice are, "This is Lukachukai" (289), as she and Set arrive at the place where he will consummate his fate. For the rest of the narrative, we are told *Set's* perceptions of Grey's transformation: "She stood and moved and talked differently. Here, in her mother's home, she assumed an atti-tude of deep propriety, dignity. With Set she could still tease and joke and whisper words in her old diction, but now she spoke quietly, in a plain and simple way, and her language was made of rhythms and silences that he had not heard before" (291).

Grey's loss of voice at this crucial point in the narrative signifies a trivialization of her character's power, possibly because of Set's need to control it. Her role at this point in Set's transformation is to become voiceless and pregnant. Like the silencing of Porcingula's laughter during her pregnancy as she "is given up" to Francisco in *House Made of Dawn*, the silencing of Grey emblemizes the need of men to devalue and thus exert control over the transgressive. Sig-nificantly, the text equates her medicine powers with her fertility. Michelle Rosaldo notes that "women as wives, mothers, witches, midwives, nuns, or whores, are defined almost exclusively in terms of their sexual functions" (31). Phallocratic power structure consigns women's value to their reproductive abilities, while allowing men a much larger range of creativity precisely because, as Bryan Turner argues, "the feminine body is the main challenge to the continuity of property and power" (37). Sherry Ortner recalls Simone de Beauvoir's statement that "woman's body seems to doom her to mere reproduction of life," an internal process, while men's value can be valorized externally and thus more visibly (75).

The objectification of the female body as sex object reaches its most extreme form in the sex scenes of both novels. With the women seen only as objects, sex is always something being done *to* them in spite of, or perhaps because of, their superficial boldness. "What will you do to me?" Angela asks Abel during their lovemaking in *House Made of Dawn*. The objectification reaches extreme limits in Dwight Dicks's rape of Grey in *The Ancient Child*, but it exists even in the more mutually erotic scenes between Grey and Billy: "Uh, Billy, will you—uh, make love to me, please?" and, in the most blatantly misogynistic line of either novel, "And then, *with infinite mercy* [my emphasis], he inserted his cock into her cunt" (97). The by now rather limp idea suggested by this statement is that women are unworthy receptacles for a man's most valued possession, his penis, that women suffer from the lack of a penis, thus the truly noble man will end women's suffering.

The objectification of women's bodies and the concept of sex as something being done to a woman are startling similar to what Susan Griffin refers to as "the metaphysics of pornography" (14). In all of the scenes of sex in both novels, the women's bodies and reactions are described in detail, but there is no corresponding description of the men's bodies or their emotional reactions, as if the men are physically present but emotionally absent. At one point, Abel holds Millie away from him so that he can see her response, then the text says, "he was brutal with her" (*House Made of Dawn* 101). The women are satisfied sexually, but if the men feel any arousal at all, the text does not mention it. Like the pornographers of Griffin's study, they "make love without feeling love" (Griffin 56).

At the core of pornography is the belief that women must be mastered by men and that women desire mastery. The pornographer is obsessed with the idea of female transgression that must be brought under control, so he fashions woman's body as a form of possession. In this fashioning, the female body must be amenable to his desires.

The sex scenes of Momaday's novels describe each of the women's bodies by the same word: "supple." The application of this word to the bodies of Angela, Millie, Pony, Porcingula, Alais, and Grey cannot be accidental; all of these women indicate their willingness to be bent to the desires of men. Only Lola is not described as "supple," but she demonstrates her suppleness in the bizarre cartwheel scene.

To the pornographer, woman's sexuality is dangerous, so he objectifies her body in order that he not be overwhelmed by it. He must control his desire, because his coldness = control = power, by allowing him to punish or reward the female body. Presumably, the "infinite mercy" that Billy displays towards Grey could become "infinitely unmerciful" were she to displease him. When Angela rejects Father Olguin through the control of her laughter, it is a transgressive act; when men exert control of their emotions in sex, it is a fitting revenge against disorderly women. Such a sense of "detachment at the core of experience" is a result of the opposition of nature and culture, and pornography is culture's revenge against nature (Griffin 66).

At the root of the devaluation of women and the view of woman as transgressor is the tendency of phallocentrism to view difference as inherently dichotomous. In *The Daughter's Seduction,* Jane Gallop asks if it is possible to consider difference without constituting an opposition. In the binary schemata underlying patriarchy, the answer is no, or at least that we have not yet found such a reality. But if we attempt, as Cixous, Trinh T. Minh-ha, and other feminist theorists suggest, an exploration of difference that proceeds from nondualistic multiplicity of thought, then we have the opportunity to create a worldview that emphasizes the integrity of difference. Questions of opposition between culture and nature, activity and passivity, logos and pathos, male and female, are superfluous if such oppositions are viewed as complementary and lacking gender specificity.

When Grey takes Set to Lukachukai, she describes it as *hozhon'i,* a place of great beauty. In the Navajo sense of the word, beauty represents goodness, happiness, health, harmony. According to Gary Witherspoon, "The Navajo does not look for beauty; he generates it within himself and projects it onto the universe" (Witherspoon 98). So, we should note, does she. This search for harmony and balance underscores traditional Native American ontology and inscribes its literature.

Abel and Set are both suffering dis-ease as a result of the disharmony and im-balance of their lives. The cure is a return to tradition through the healing powers of myth, story, and song, rooted in a particular landscape, so the healing agents are to be found only in a return to ancestral land and voices. Rain, the metaphor of healing in the Night Chant, is both male and female. "House made of male rain / House made of dark mist / House made of female rain." To achieve balance, nature requires both male and female. They are complements; one is not more essential than the other. The goal is to surround oneself in beauty so that "In beauty it is finished."

In *House Made of Dawn* and *The Ancient Child,* Momaday tells deeply moving stories of Abel's and Set's journeys to beauty. Both men are rendered voiceless by their lack of identity in a community, so the plea of the Night Chant to "restore my voice to me" would be poignant except that the restoration of their voices comes at the expense of female voices. Abel and Set both achieve a reconciliation with their individual and tribal identities, so the novels purport to be an affirmation in language of the human and tribal spirit.

It is disturbing, however, that their reconciliation occurs in spite of mostly negative forces given female form, as if to suggest that the feminine must be denied or overcome in order for a male to achieve his healing. The characterization of contemporary women in Momaday's novels demonstrates a lack of harmony and balance, an underlying misogyny. Women are generally negative, manipulative, duplicitous, possessive, perverse, and transgressive; therefore, they must be objectified and commodified. Even more disturbingly, women readers are invited to participate in this objectification and commodification through Fetterley's process of immasculation. In his representation of female characters, Momaday subverts sacred myths, stories, and songs to the profane purpose of devaluing women. As a result, the sense of harmony and balance and *hozhon'i* achieved by the male protagonists is hollow and meaningless unless the feminine is also valorized.

4

OWNING MOURNING DOVE

The Dynamics of Authenticity

On the morning of August 15, 1936, seventy-five-year-old Lucullus Virgil McWhorter picked up his newspaper, *The Spokesman Review,* and discovered on the back page a brief story reporting the death the previous week of his long-time friend and collaborator, Mourning Dove, an Okanogon Indian woman whose first book, the 1927 historical romance *Cogewea,* he had edited. Immediately, McWhorter, a Yakima, Washington, businessman, historian, and Indian-rights activist, sat down at his typewriter and wrote a letter of condolence to Mourning Dove's husband, Fred Galler, of Omak, Washington, expressing his grief and shock at the loss of a woman he had considered a daughter. In addition to expressing his personal grief, he lamented the silencing of her voice in her writing, a voice that had sympathetically rendered the experience of the Okanogon people during a painful transitional period in their history as they were forced by federal Indian policy into a system of private landownership and a way of life based on agriculture.

The opening paragraph of McWhorter's letter to Galler says everything that a proper condolence letter should say. In the next paragraph, however, the tone changes somewhat as the persona of McWhorter, the editor and entrepreneur, begins to emerge, making a bid to edit Mourning Dove's remaining unpublished manuscript. Finally, having moved his thoughts from genuine grief to opportunism, McWhorter makes a callously timed request of Galler to return books on loan to Mourning Dove.

Written some twenty years after they first met in Walla Walla at a Frontier's Day celebration, this letter sums up the complexities of the relationship between Mourning Dove and McWhorter, a relationship that even today resists categorization. If he considered her his daughter, she made it equally clear that he was like a father to her. While she frequently chafed at his editorial demands, she was capable of insisting on her own way or of reaching a compromise. If he sometimes appeared to be exploiting her, she recognized his usefulness. Finally, their friendship endured for more than twenty years in a cultural environment of racial animus, resulting in the publication of a novel that is generally considered to be one of the first written by a Native American woman, a novel that prefigures contemporary Native writing by and about mixed-bloods and their problematic search for identity.

The "collaboration" between Mourning Dove and McWhorter raises troubling questions about the nature of authorship and authenticity in an intercultural project, about the ethics of a Euro-American's intrusions into an indigenous person's text, about the changes in inflection in a woman's text when the editor is a man. Most importantly, it raises the question of how and if a woman of color maintains her agency in her dealings with the dominant culture. Many critics argue that Mourning Dove did not, in fact, maintain agency in the McWhorter relationship, that her voice was subsumed and compromised by the frequency and insistence of his voice in her writing. To a certain extent, this is an accurate assessment. One needs only to go looking for Mourning Dove's papers to recognize the partial validity of this view, for there is no repository of her papers under her name in any library. All of her extant letters and manuscripts are catalogued in the collection of McWhorter's papers at Washington State University in Pullman, while a few others are in the papers of anthropologist Erna Gunther, whom Mourning Dove never met, at the University of Washington in Seattle.

Mourning Dove was a pivotal figure in the development of Native American literature. The structure of her novel marries two literary genres—the nineteenth-century tradition of the sentimental romance and the Western adventure novel, especially the dime novel, with its stereotypical characters and clear delineation of morality. Yet *Cogewea's* use of the Okanogon oral tradition as an organic plot element marks the text as structurally innovative and subversive in its resistance to the conventional view of Indians as a dying race of noble savages.

Despite the novel's obvious structural innovations, the debate over McWhorter's editorial role has overshadowed the critical discussion of its literary merits. Mary V. Dearborn's *Pocahontas's Daughters: Gender and Ethnicity in American Culture* is one of the first critical studies to take the novel seriously, but she finds the text "slightly schizophrenic" (20), describing it as "less a novel than a bizarrely textured pastiche," and asking, "[C]ould one person be responsible for such a pastiche?" (21). Charles E. Larson's *American Indian Fiction* relegates *Cogewea* to the appendix because of its double-voiced narration. Jay Miller, the editor of Mourning Dove's "autobiography," itself an extremely problematic text, relates rumors spread by a Bureau of Indian Affairs official on her own reservation that Mourning Dove had merely allowed her name to appear on McWhorter's text to lend authenticity. Dexter Fisher's introduction to the University of Nebraska reprint notes that the novel "sags at times under the weight of [McWhorter's] vituperation" (xiv).

It was not until the scholarship of Alanna Kathleen Brown in the 1980s that the relationship between McWhorter and Mourning Dove came under systematic and sympathetic scrutiny through a detailed and painstaking examination of their twenty-year unpublished correspondence. Brown's work acknowledges that McWhorter "ultimately co-authored the work," resulting in "serious inconsistencies in both plot and voice" ("Mourning Dove" 3); having conceded the textual weaknesses at the outset, however, Brown moves the discussion to more important matters: Mourning Dove's celebration of the mixed-blood as a new people and her pioneering integration of the Okanogon oral tradition into a written literary genre. Brown's scholarship properly spotlights the letters between Mourning Dove and McWhorter as the most reliable narrative of their relationship. Over the course of more than twenty years, the two principals were face to face on only a few occasions; it seems entirely appropriate, then, that a relationship constructed on words should be almost completely inscribed by words.

For most of her life, Mourning Dove was faced with conflicting claims on her time and talent, from ne'er-do-well husbands and would-be anthropologists to the skepticism of her own tribal community. The demands on her, both physical and mental, were so great that in a letter to McWhorter dated 27 December 1921, she was moved to write, "when I get rich I am going to build me a typee of my own for a writing room where I can lock myself in and write each day for an hour. a sacred hour it will be. Where I can be alone to my hobbys [sic]." This poignant letter was written eight years before Virginia Woolf expressed a similar longing for time and space, but with the added need for five hundred pounds a year, a sum of money beyond Mourning Dove's imagining. Mourning Dove's life was always owned by other people and responsibilities. Even today she is, in a very real sense, owned by other people.

Mourning Dove was born circa 1888 and christened Christine Quintasket, just four years before historian Frederick Jackson Turner declared the frontier closed and, with it, the first chapter in the life of the American nation. She was born into a context of competing, opposing stories: the Anglo-American fiction of "the existence of an area of free land" combined with Turner's frontier thesis of its "continuous recession" versus the Native American reality of invasion and conquest of ancestral land and a culture in transition. In *Mourning Dove: A Salishan Autobiography* she writes of her gratitude at being born "a descendant of the genuine Americans, the Indians," and being born at a time when she could know Indian people who still lived as part of the traditional Okanogon culture, hunting and fishing at a time of enormous governmental pressure to farm (3).

Even the circumstances of her birth were appropriate to her sense of being caught between two worlds. She relates that she was born in a canoe as her mother and grandmother crossed the Kootenay River, and she was swaddled in the commercially produced plaid shirt of the oarsman. While her account of her lineage is disputed by tribal records, she states that her mother, Lucy Stui-kin, was a full-blood; her father, Joseph Quintasket, was a mixed-blood, born to a Nicola mother and a Scots father. The eldest of seven children, Mourning Dove's education was erratic, consisting of a few years of mission and Bureau of Indian Affairs schooling, which ended at her mother's death in 1902, and a year at a Calgary business school when she was older. However, she received a substantial education in traditional Okanogon ways from a female elder, a woman named Teequalt, whom Mourning Dove found wandering in the woods and who was subsequently taken into the family by Mourning Dove's mother. Teequalt, on whom Mourning Dove modeled the character of the Stemteemä in *Cogewea,* told the children stories and undertook the spiritual, moral, and traditional training of the girls in the family. As Mourning Dove relates in her autobiography, her mother had little use for white education and preferred her daughters to remain close to her and to Teequalt.

Despite the irregularity of her formal education, Mourning Dove developed a passion for reading through the "yellowback novels" brought into her home by Jimmy Ryan, a young white boy adopted by her parents. While we have no way of knowing which specific dime novels she read, we can assume that she read the most popular ones of the day with their heroic or anti-heroic construction of the sheriff, outlaw, or detective, and their use of the frontier as trope for addressing the social problems of the emerging American metropolis— class conflicts between labor and capital, populism and progressivism (Slotkin 127). Ironically, Mourning Dove and Jimmy Ryan, Indian and white, in a setting only recently dubbed "the frontier," found escape reading texts that used the very setting in which they lived their lives as an allegory for the problems of the cities from which they were far removed.

When Mourning Dove met McWhorter in 1915, she had already drafted a version of *Cogewea*, her own rendition of the dime novel, but McWhorter's early editorial desires had little to do with her novel. Instead, he saw her as the cultural insider who could collect traditional Okanogon stories before they disappeared forever. Recognizing, perhaps, Mourning Dove's susceptibility to a good story, one of McWhorter's first letters to her, dated 29 November 1915, is framed like an oral story told in the stereotypical voice of the mystic Native of the white imagination, addressing her as "Mourning Dove of the Okanogons" and referring to himself as the "Old Wolf of the Yakimas." Having established his rhetorical stance and himself as a figure of authority, McWhorter re-creates Mourning Dove, the flesh and blood woman, as a fictional character in a story of his own making as he describes his vision of the forking path of the future for the Okanogons. In his vision, the traditions and stories of the tribes are now maintained only by the elders, who are approaching death. Then the character of Mourning Dove, potential savior of traditions and stories, enters the narrative.

When the fictional Mourning Dove sees the dilemma facing her, she ponders her course of action. She, too, has a vision, actually a vision within a vision, that carries her beyond the impending death of the elders to a vision of a paradisiacal past. She must choose between the dividing trails: one easy trail leads to cultural oblivion; the other, more difficult trail leads to cultural immortality. McWhorter appeals to Mourning Dove's innate desire to be of service to her people, implying as well that only she can save them.

The promise of immortality that McWhorter equates with the future clearly is both tribal and individual. Ironically, McWhorter tries to reconcile for Mourning Dove the tensions he knows she feels about preserving the traditions of her people, traditions that emphasized communalism, by appealing to her individualistic desire for immortality. Thus, he effectively collapses the dualism of indigenous valorization of communalism and American valorization of individualism, trying to preserve that which is vanishing with the value system of the usurper.

Nowhere in this lengthy letter does McWhorter mention her novelistic goals. His concern is solely with her ability, by virtue of being a cultural insider, to collect and record stories told by her people. Nowhere in the letter does he acknowledge the compromising position he is placing her in with her people, or the slippery ethics of collecting such information in order for it to be published and disseminated to cultural outsiders. For him, preservation means everything because he believes the tribes are doomed. The fact that Mourning Dove aspires to excel in a Western literary genre breaks the conventional rules for what a Native woman should aspire to. As Trinh T. Minh-ha observes, "The place of the native is always well-delimitated. . . . Otherness has its laws and interdictions" (*When the Moon Waxes Red* 69). Under this paradigm, the choice of genre and subject matter permissible to Mourning Dove must be of McWhorter's devising. As a Native woman, she is privy to information that an outsider is not; therefore, her choices are limited. She is expected to know the oral traditions of her people, not written literary forms.

Mourning Dove's response to McWhorter's letter also makes no mention of her novel, adopting a similar elevated rhetorical style, but also expressing both her confidence in him personally and her doubts about the sincerity of any white man. That Mourning Dove's response to McWhorter should be double-voiced, avowing her trust in him while at the same time reminding him of the centuries of betrayal that inscribe their developing relationship, demonstrates her acute understanding of the cultural history which encodes them. That McWhorter, in effect, calls Mourning Dove into being in his highly stylized "vision" is also consistent with repeated first ethnographic encounters between Western men and indigenous women. The dynamics of the relationship between Mourning Dove and McWhorter, as revealed in their early correspondence, follow the paradigm articulated by Deborah Kodish in which the first encounter between the folklorist, usually a young and powerful male, and the folk is described as an almost magical event. In the next step of Kodish's paradigm, the folk are cast as repositories of an endless supply of stories and songs. Then the folk, usually women, through the efforts of the folklorist, are reminded of the value of their culture. Finally, the emphasis returns to the feeling of the folklorist in the encounter, with the feeling of the folk left unexpressed. As Kodish remarks, "these accounts resonate with a marked, if unacknowledged, sexuality. Male collectors appear as powerful, magical outsiders, folktale heroes initiating action and reestablishing value. Female informants appear as passive vehicles, unwitting receptacles of knowledge, silent, unspeaking, to be wooed and won into speech" (574–75).

At the time of McWhorter's letter to her, Mourning Dove was approximately twenty-seven years old, and McWhorter was fifty-four. Even though he does not fit Kodish's description of the *youthful* male outsider, he does fit the description of the power residing in the *knowledgeable* outsider. The work of Michel Foucault has made abundantly explicit the historical correspondence between systems of knowledge and systems of power. Certainly, McWhorter possessed knowledge that was beyond Mourning Dove's circumstances at that time—namely knowledge about language and how to transform language into print for a reading audience. To a person of marginal education, McWhorter appeared to have the magical power to transform words into books, and as he himself made clear in his letters, he had many friends who also possessed this knowledge/power and who could be of service to her. Given the experience of her tribe and others with the American legal system, Mourning Dove also knew that printed words have power so extraordinary that they can separate Indian children from their parents and can transform communal land into small plots staked along a straight line, permitting individuals to own these plots and to exclude those who do not own them, all based on words on a crucial piece of paper known as a *title*.

Another aspect of McWhorter's vision that imbued him with power is his construction of Mourning Dove in temporal and spatial distance, an integral part of the process of Other-ing. McWhorter articulates his vision in the first person, present tense when he speaks of himself, saying, "I am," "I see," "I look," and "I want," the introductory words of six of the eight paragraphs of his early letter. Even as these paragraphs begin with an emphasis on his actions in present time, he also implies a distance between himself and the object of his actions—the woman of his vision. He operates in present time, while she operates within mythic time, a spatial distancing that is one of the trademarks of colonialism. Even the old people of his vision, although their actions are described in present-tense verbs, are spatially removed into a mythic past. This distancing device is described by Johannes Fabian as a "denial of coevalness," which is "a persistent and systematic tendency to place the referent(s) of anthropology in a Time other than the present of the producer of anthropological discourse" (31). And, as Fabian argues, the denial of coevalness is fundamental, not just to particular modes of anthropology, but to its very existence.

By situating his subjects in the past or, at least, in a mythic present very far removed both spatially and temporally from his discursive present, McWhorter indulges in a common tendency of colonialism to mourn for what has been lost. Described by Renato Rosaldo as "imperialist nostalgia" for the "traditional" culture—that is, the condition of the culture when the agents of colonialism first encountered it—such nostalgia freezes the culture in time, as if it has always been the way it was at first contact, in an immutable and mythic present. In Western anthropological discourse, such cultural reification occurs only among "primitive," nontechnological, and oral cultures. As Rosaldo points out, however, these very same agents of colonialism are responsible for the transformation (read as "loss") of the culture in the first place. By denying coevalness, this account fails to provide for an understanding of how the culture has changed on its own terms, either through a natural internal progression or through contact with other "primitive" cultures. As Rosaldo argues, "Imperialist nostalgia revolves around a paradox: A person kills somebody, and then mourns the victim. In more attenuated forms, someone deliberately alters a form of life, and then regrets that things have not remained as they were prior to the intervention" (*Culture and Truth* 69–70). And, as Rosaldo notes, imperialist nostalgia is also closely linked to that outgrowth of progress, " 'the white man's burden,' where civilized nations stand duty-bound to uplift so-called savage ones" (70). In a progressively changing world, a "static" society, such as a "primitive" one, serves as a convenient reference point for the one in flux, a measure of what has been lost, and what has been gained. Rosaldo points out that "when the so-called civilizing process destabilizes forms of life, the agents of change experience transformations of other cultures as if they were personal losses" (70).

The concept of imperialist nostalgia goes far in explaining McWhorter's zeal in convincing Mourning Dove to record her tribal stories before they were lost. In his vision, it is *he* who can read the doomed future of the tribes; *he* who sees that their only hope is the young woman of his vision; and *he* who makes her duty plain to her. In other words, *he* is the true savior of the tribes. The conquering culture kills and then resuscitates.

McWhorter approached his obligation as a friend of the Indian with a missionary zeal all too common among humanitarians of his day, whose desire to preserve the remnants of Native cultures, after years of decimation by whites, was rooted in a resistance to progressivism and Darwinism. As Robert Berkhofer notes, the basic incompatibility of white and Native cultures gave rise to whites' perception of Indians as a threat when alive, but whose demise was an occasion for nostalgia (29). Further, as James Clifford points out, this nostalgia for what the dominant culture perceives as disappeared or disappearing is frequently located in the process of inscribing a previously oral culture into a written culture, where knowledge that had historically been held in common now becomes the intellectual property of an individual (*Writing Culture* 118). It is not coincidental that the concept of intellectual property, which began in the late eighteenth century, and the concept of place as property, as applied in the Dawes Act of 1887, are separated by a mere one hundred years.

Formally titled the General Allotment Act, but popularly known as the Dawes Act after the Massachusetts senator who helped achieve its passage through Congress, this law called for the division of reservation lands into private parcels of 160 acres to be homesteaded by Indian people; after twenty-five years, patent for the land and citizenship would accrue to the Native homesteader.

Both the concept of intellectual property and place as property arise from the developing sense of possessive individualism that began in the West in the seventeenth century with the emergence of a sense of the Self as owner. As Clifford notes, during this time "the ideal individual surround[ed] itself with accumulated properties and goods" as a sign of having a "culture." Clifford argues that the very act of collecting presupposes a prior act of assigning value and meaning ("Objects" 237). In McWhorter's case, he was collecting the oral culture of a people, and with collection comes the arbitrary assignment of value and meaning. Value and meaning, to a large extent, arise from the authenticity of that which is collected. Authenticity, however, is a problematic term when used to describe cultures, because it presupposes a dualism of authentic/inauthentic that is closely linked to notions of culture, time, and identity.

James Clifford's definition of culture emphasizes its current dialogism. Culture is process, not product; ongoing, not static. But this concept of culture is a relatively recent construct. In the mid-nineteenth century's enormous social disruption, culture was viewed as the universal conclusion of an evolutionary process that resulted in an autonomous individual. But by 1900, Clifford argues, evolutionary progressivism was waning, and a new concept of culture arose emphasizing plurality of meaning and value, with a corresponding change in the concept of universal autonomous individualism to a more localized knowledge of the Self in relation to a specific community.

By the twentieth century, a recognition of the plurality of cultures and values emerged as an alternative to racist classification of an increasingly complex global interconnectedness (*Predicament of Culture* 92–93, 234). In this formulation, " 'culture' is always relational, an inscription of communicative processes that exist, historically, *between* subjects in relations of power" (Introduction 15). This reformulation of "culture" is also closely linked to the collection of artifacts and oral traditions in which the possessive Self creates taxonomies of authenticity and thus of value on what is collected. As Clifford notes, by the early twentieth century this more inclusive definition of culture resulted in the elevation to the status of "art" of an increasing number of exotic and primitive artifacts, a category which includes the oral culture of a people.

The concept of authenticity is also closely linked to the ethno-

graphic construction of time and the categorization of primitive artifacts as art. Only the "pure" unadulterated culture was capable of producing "authentic" artifacts. McWhorter's charge to Mourning Dove
was to capture and preserve the "primitive simplicity" of her people,
as if she could inscribe their essence before it had been ruined by the
complexities of "civilization." To be truly authentic, the stories had to
be accurate as only the elders could render them accurate, but the
accuracy was to be determined by the literate agent of civilization—
himself. McWhorter equates age with authenticity, which is another
form of cultural reification, or what Clifford terms "ethnographic pastoralism," a form of "salvage ethnography" in which primitive cultures
are always locked into a future that is already past, and the past is the
only authentic tradition, but the past, traditional society "is weak and
needs to be represented by an outsider. . . . The recorder and inter-
preter of fragile custom is custodian of an essence, unimpeachable
witness to an authenticity"—an authenticity that conveniently cannot
be refuted, because it is in the past ("On Ethnographic Allegory" 113).

Since, in the ethnographer's establishment of the discipline's authority, it is always the ethnographer who brings writing to bear in
cultural preservation, literacy is associated with civilization; orality,
with primitivism. In the West, Clifford notes, "the passage from oral
to literate is a potent recurring *story*—of power, corruption, loss"
(118). And, as Rosaldo argues, the pastoral mode, deriving as it does
from courtly tradition, is itself a literary representation of systems of
dominance by patronizingly promoting a "reverence for a simplicity
'we' have lost," and creating an interactive hegemony "between town
and country, middle class and working class, and colonizer and colonized" ("From the Door" 96, 97). Change is configured as disorder as
"All the beautiful, primitive places are ruined" (Clifford, *Predicament
of Culture* 4); if the pure is changing and thus becoming tainted, there
is no going back, no essence to recall.

McWhorter demanded of Mourning Dove that she be the authentic Indian, the purveyor of authentic folklore, while failing to acknowledge that she operated out of two cultures, one oral and tribal,
the other literate and Westernized. He denies her coevalness; she
cannot change. At the same time, however, he relies on her capacity

to change by becoming a modern literate woman. He expects her to be "one of the pure products of America," while simultaneously exhibiting the characteristics of the impure, an impossible position for her. Clifford quotes William Carlos Williams's poem *Spring and All*, whose opening lines are acutely appropriate to the role McWhorter assigns to Mourning Dove: "The pure products of America / go crazy" (Introduction 1).

In her letters to McWhorter, Mourning Dove frequently expressed frustration at the bifurcated sense of identity her liminal position created. In a letter dated 9 February 1915, she remarks that she has tried to live for years by white rules but now cannot deny the call of blood, as she yearns to reject "civilization" for "the golden race." In this letter, Mourning Dove clearly chooses her Native American ancestry over her white, yet she also accepts the dualism of "civilization" versus "primitivism," as well as indulging in a bit of ethnographic pastoralism herself.

In a 1916 letter discussing the dedication of *Cogewea*, she tells McWhorter that she wants the dedication to contain no mention of her white blood, because she believes that all the credit will then accrue to her whiteness rather than her Indian-ness, even though she recognizes that her photograph (to be included in the book) reveals her to be dark enough to pass for full-blood. Even as she avows her Indian-ness, Mourning Dove relies on her photographic image, a tool of impure civilization, to authenticate and even augment her Indian ancestry. Although she herself was a mixed-blood, she preferred to pass for full-blood. Yet during this same time period, she complains to McWhorter that she has difficulty receiving mail under her Indian name, Humishuma, and asks him to address his correspondence to her by her English name. In another 1916 letter, she states unequivocally, "It is h— to be a half-breed."

Her letter of 12 September 1916 shows further conflicts in her self-identification. She tells McWhorter that she is looking forward to a planned speaking tour of the East because she feels comfortable on the stage and wishes that she could avail herself of the emerging photographic technology of either motion pictures or slides, which could demonstrate visually to her audience how most contemporary

Indians live in houses, with a few, "of the lower class," still in tipis. She also reminds McWhorter that she has done some movie acting in Spokane to promote *Cogewea.*

In this letter, Mourning Dove reinforces the fact that her Indian contemporaries used name-brand products such as Kodak, living and acting in a changing, mobile, technological, and media-conscious culture. Not only does she know the price of slides, she also knows how to produce them and understands the role of the media in advertising. She demonstrates a certain amount of class consciousness in references to modern Indians who live in houses as opposed to the "lower" classes still living in tipis. The same letter speaks of driving in a car for 35 miles and passing the setting in the novel where her heroine Cogewea is abused by her white suitor. Then Mourning Dove's business acumen emerges. Perhaps out of necessity, she insists that her expenses for the speaking tour must be advanced; furthermore, she demands to know if McWhorter has had *Cogewea* copyrighted as he had promised and states that she wants the copyright in her own (then) name of Crystal McLeod rather than in her father's name as she had originally requested.

She also expresses her mixed pleasure that McWhorter was able to provide the traditional Okanogon female head-dress for her speaking engagements — mixed pleasure because she is sure it makes her "look funny" — but she consents to wear it to please McWhorter. Because clothing, a part of the material culture of a people, is an authenticating apparatus, the great irony here is that it is transformed into performative costume by the agent of the colonial culture in order that the authenticity of the reproduction be complete; the representative of the subjugated culture, by acquiescing to wear the costume despite the fact that it feels foreign to her, completes the cycle of authentification of the colonial culture. In other words, by giving to white audiences the image of Indians they expect to see, Mourning Dove becomes a player in the cultural representation taking place, thereby subverting the reification of her Indian-ness implicit in her performance. Nevertheless, by demanding that her manuscript be copyrighted, she displays her understanding of the power of cultural inscription. She also understands that the American legal system, historically one of the most efficient tools used against Native peoples, is built upon a discursive power, and she uses the system to ensure that her own cultural inscription is safe-guarded, a transcultural process.

Mourning Dove again demonstrates how transculturation affects her discursive practices in a 1921 letter to McWhorter. Early in her writing career, she adopted the pen name "Mourning Dove," after the wife of Salmon, but always spelled it *Morning* Dove. After visiting a natural history museum in 1921, she discovered that the correct spelling contains a "u" and so asked McWhorter to make the correction on the novel's title page. "Transculturation," as used by ethnographers, refers to the ways "subordinated or marginalized groups select and invent from materials transmitted to them by the dominant or metropolitan culture" (Pratt, *Imperial Eyes* 6). In the situation involving the spelling of her name, Mourning Dove used the practice of the dominant culture to collect and then exhibit in museums what the possessive Western Self deems to be the authentic artifacts of primitive people, only in this case the artifact is a natural one rendered almost, but not quite, life-like by a taxidermist's skill, similar to the colonial culture's rendering of Indians as objects of study. Yet rather than feeling diminished by her spelling error, Mourning Dove simply states that she is still learning (reified objects do not demonstrate this sort of growth) and instructs McWhorter to make the correction.

These passages and others from her letters demonstrate the complex process of identity formation for the mixed-blood in the contact zone of competing cultures. As Clifford defines identity in the ethnographic sense, it must "always be mixed, relational and inventive" (Introduction 10). Mourning Dove's "value" to McWhorter, their friendship notwithstanding, was as Insider to a culture he believed to be in danger of extinction. What he failed to see was that his creation of Mourning Dove as Insider necessarily also created her as Outsider in an identity that was, in Trinh T. Minh-ha's words, "not quite the same, not quite the other," where she became "this inappropriate other or same who moves about always with at least two gestures: that of affirming 'I am like you' while persisting in her difference and that of reminding 'I am different' while unsettling every definition of difference arrived at" (*When the Moon Waxes Red* 76). Since no identity is unified, always subjective and relational, the Outsider is always relational to the Insider and to herself, just as the Insider is always relational to the Outsider and to herself.

While Mourning Dove acquiesced to many of McWhorter's demands concerning her work, her letters also reveal a conflicted but supremely inventive woman who resourcefully adapted from the colonizing culture what was most useful to her. Her inventiveness, combined with a shrewd ability to successfully maneuver through the minefield of cultural differences, reveals the power implicit in her liminality. In all of her negotiations through the "Not you/Like you" maze, she never perceived herself solely as a victim of poverty, race, gender, or historical circumstance, although she was, of course, a victim of each. Her poverty forced her into jobs that strained her health and drained her energy for writing, such as migrant work in the apple orchards, cooking for a migrant labor camp, and working as a boardinghouse proprietress. Born during a transitional time for Native peoples, she successfully made the transition from traditional Okanogon life to the contemporary world of Indians who owned property, farmed, and used the developing technology of telephones, typewriters, automobiles, and photography. She not only witnessed but also contributed to the process whereby the Okanogons moved from an oral to a literate culture, without losing the entirety of the oral culture. As a mixed-blood, she maneuvered between an indigenous world and a white world—neither of which could completely encompass her—and experienced the conflicted identity of a person in such a position.

Belonging wholly in neither culture, Mourning Dove could select, to the degree her poverty afforded her, from each what was most advantageous. She was enough of a white woman to recognize the advantages of writing down traditional stories to prevent their loss in a world rapidly embracing literacy, yet she was enough of an Indian to recognize that her exoticism as a writing Native was appealing to a white reading public. The power of this liminality she brought to bear selectively in her dealings with McWhorter, acquiescing to his editorial decisions in some instances but holding her ground on others she considered crucial. For example, she refused his suggestion to change the ending of the novel. He preferred to have Cogewea die, befitting her status as a member of a "dying" race; Mourning Dove, however, insisted on her version, in which Cogewea, having been abused and abandoned to die by her unscrupulous white lover, Alfred Densmore (whose interest in Cogewea had been flamed by stories of her reputed wealth), triumphs in the end by surviving and marrying the mixed-blood man Jim LaGrinder, who has patiently loved her all along. Shortly after the wedding, Cogewea inherits a large sum of money from her long-lost father, and an impoverished Alfred Densmore reads of her good fortune in a newspaper in a run-down Eastern boardinghouse. In a nicely ironic touch, Mourning Dove acknowledges the power of the printed word to redress a wrongful deed, just as her experience as a Native woman has witnessed the power of the printed word to create and legitimize injustice.

Although we may never know with any certainty why she permitted McWhorter such an obvious presence in her text, one possibility may be that his editorial intrusions, which readers today find so annoying, did not appear unusual to her. Throughout her life, the concept of property remained somewhat foreign to her. Certainly she desired to lead a more comfortable life than the one she was living, but nowhere in the letters does she mention the desire to *accumulate* property. She daydreams, perhaps half-heartedly, that the novel will make her rich, but the only things she mentions that she truly wants from this future wealth is time to write without distraction and a writing place of her own. The only other things she mentions from time to time are a new typewriter and ribbons, and an endless supply of paper. These are rather modest desires. Throughout her life she generously took into her home several children and raised them as her own, just as her parents had done. And just as her parents had difficulty accepting the Western construction of land as property, perhaps Mourning Dove had difficulty accepting the equally Western construction of intellectual property created and owned solely by an individual.

Mourning Dove grew up in a family and a tribal community that emphasized communalism, not individualism. To be sure, these values in both her family and her community were in a transitional state, but the early training she received at home from her mother and, especially, from Teequalt rested on a tradition of learning to value community through sharing the necessities of life through the medium of oral storytelling. In addition, traditional Okanogon values emphasized pacifism and gender equality. Conflict was not valued in her community's emphasis on harmony achieved through a dialogic storytelling medium. While stories and songs in tribal communities are composed by individuals, much of their meaning derives from the interactive nature of the performance context. Tribal communities do not necessarily perceive the composer of the songs or stories as a unified subject in the Foucaudian notion of the author as owner of that which s/he creates. As Foucault points out, the individualization of the "author-function" relationship is not universal across cultures and discourses, but is a historical construct of the late eighteenth to early nineteenth centuries, when the complex legal codification of systems of property, including property rights, was established. Foucault notes as well that this assignment of ownership of texts as the property of individuals occurred partially to make the author subject to punishment by the State if the ideas—the property—were deemed transgressive by the State ("What Is an Author" 346–47). It should also be noted that the construction of the Author as a unified subject occurred at the historical conjunction of the notion of the possessive Self with the nineteenth-century removal of Indian peoples from ancestral land, culminating in the establishment of the allotment system, the conceptual and legal translation of place into property.

Deriving from a culture that had great difficulty perceiving either land or ideas as private property, it is conceivable that Mourning Dove considered McWhorter's editorial inclusions of chapter epigraphs, ethnographic material, and political diatribe to be meritorious contributions to the text. In her letter of 4 June 1928 she expresses her surprise at some of the changes he made but concludes, "I think they are fine, and you made a tasty dressing like a cook would do, with a fine meal. . . . I felt like it was someone elses [sic] book and not mine at all. In fact, the finishing touches are put there by you, and I have never seen it."

Some critics who have reviewed the correspondence point to this letter as proof that McWhorter had appropriated Mourning Dove's text as his own. I suggest, however, that this interpretation requires reading a degree of anger and resentment into her words where none was intended. I suggest that instead of anger or resentment at his changes, she is complimenting him in a metaphor very familiar to her—food preparation—and that she is sharing authorship with him. In a later letter she continues to be very complimentary, acknowledging that her book would not have been as worthwhile without his contributions.

What Mourning Dove and McWhorter created in *Cogewea* was a polyphonic novel, with a dialogic interplay of voices that Bakhtin describes as "heteroglossia." In Bakhtin's formulation of the modern novel genre, the novel becomes the site of seriously contested codes of pluralistic cultural meaning. *Cogewea,* as polyphonic novel, derives its complexities of language and culture not simply from the fractured modernity of the novel genre, but also from the interplay of voices and textures of the oral tradition with its multiple narrative versions, and the exchange between performer and audience that creates the meaning of an oral performance, while implicitly denying a singular, unified authorship. The potential shift in meaning from one performance to another, as teller and audience shift, prevents meaning from becoming static, and so maintains the vitality of the storytelling process. Perhaps Mourning Dove recognized that the multiple voices of her text would ensure its survival.

Ultimately, what endures in the novel is of Mourning Dove's creation, while McWhorter's contributions ironically appear frozen in a quaint time warp. The epigraphs he cherished are drawn from writers no longer considered major figures. The ethnographic insertions are as boring as the worst ethnographic writing can be. Cogewea's lapses in diction are so stilted as to be humorous. And the polemics against political figures and institutions, while still retaining some sting, are directed at individuals and issues long forgotten. But the subjective elements of the novel—the romance between Mourning Dove and her two suitors, the descriptions of the beautiful Montana landscape, her inscription of specific oral stories such as the tragedy of Green Blanket Feet, and Cogewea's search for identity in a rapidly changing world—are what bring the novel to life. McWhorter's contributions, which were intended as a brake to Mourning Dove's sentimentality, and which probably were crucial to the novel's publication, now seem to be annoying distractions from the real story. Changing times and shifting literary tastes have relegated McWhorter's contributions to the category of propaganda.

It is tempting to read the novel, as many have done, as one more example of the silencing of the Native woman's voice by the invading (male) culture. It is equally tempting to read the novel as an example of Indian women's resistance to, and triumph over, attempts to dominate and silence them. Both readings would be oversimplifications of a vastly complex process of gendered and racial collaboration and friendship in a politically charged situation. Ultimately, the letters reveal two very different individuals trying to negotiate their differences with respect, friendship, frequent frustration, and occasional humor, against a historical backdrop of conquest, betrayal, and resistance.

5

STORYTELLING WOMEN

Paula Gunn Allen and Toni Morrison

"All that time, all that time, I thought I was missing Jude." And the loss pressed down on her chest and came up into her throat. "We was girls together," she said as though explaining something. "O Lord, Sula," she cried, "girl, girl, girlgirlgirl."
—Toni Morrison, Sula

Over the last several years, numerous literary and cultural theorists—Todorov, Clifford, Said, Anzaldúa, Trinh, and Spivak, to name but a few—have addressed the problematic tendency of the dominant culture to view people of color as a monolithic Other, a concept which is frequently female-gendered. We are advised as well to question the validity of the term "dominant culture" with its usual male-gendering. But for women of color, the marginalization implicit in Other-ness is a double-edged sword. One very positive result of the insistence by women of color on the specificity of their cultural and gendered experience is that by denying the monolithism of both the Other and the dominant culture, they reinscribe their cultural and individual identity. This reinscription raises several questions, however. In our critical valorization of specificity, are we in danger of denying the possibility of commonality in cultural and aesthetic expression? Are specificity and commonality mutually exclusive? Does an emphasis on specificity at the expense of commonality risk further dividing women of color, in particular, who in their historic exclusion from voice are the victims of a dual oppression?

Two preeminent contemporary women writers explore these issues in their fiction through their representation of femaleness in their respective cultures. Paula Gunn Allen, a Laguna/Sioux/Anglo writer, describes her complex novel *The Woman Who Owned the Shadows* as a confluence, a road, a vision quest, a musical composition, and "a series of small suicides, some of which are fatal" (qtd. in Crawford et al. 99). These same metaphors describe Toni Morrison's equally complex *Sula*. A close examination of the novels reveals multiple parallels in the representation of the ways in which, for women, the crucial search for individual and cultural identity and voice is shaped by the Native American and African American oral traditions, and by the relationship of landscape to human action, thus providing at least a jumping off point for women of all races to consider what they have in common as well as what divides them.

That Allen's *The Woman Who Owned the Shadows* is the story of Ephanie's search for identity is self-evident. What distinguishes her identity quest from numerous others are the complicating factors of gender, place, race, class, spirituality, and sexuality. She is a woman who initially defines herself in relation to the men in her life: the husband who abandons her; Stephen who smothers her; and Thomas who uses her femaleness and Indian-ness to keep his own pain as a Nisei at bay. She needs men to authenticate her reality; when they inevitably fail, she must question the reality and purpose of her existence. She also lacks a grounding in a particular place, moving in meaningless circles between Albuquerque, San Francisco, Oregon, and Colorado. As a mixed-blood, she has ties to both the Indian and the Anglo community but belongs wholly in neither. Like her native Southwest, she is a confluence of cultures and attitudes. Even her name, Ephanie, wars with her physical appearance. "Ephanie was for someone tall and serene. Someone filled with grace. But like her it was a split name, a name half of this and half of that: Epiphany. Effie. An almost name. An almost event" (3).

In interviews, Allen has elaborated the meaning of shadows in her work. Shadows are both good and bad places, representing fear, the shadowy unfocused area of her mind, but they also represent coolness, shade, the land of the dead that sends the rain, and a state of in-between—"half-breed" (qtd. in Bruchac 14). For Ephanie to own the shadows, she must come to terms with what it means to be female in a man's world, white in a tribal culture, Indian in a white culture, shaman in a technological world, and lesbian in the midst of homophobia. Because she resists categorization, she risks the loss of sanity and life. Like her grandmother, Shimanna (Nightshade), who marries a "squawman" and is for ever an-Other, outside the borders of both worlds, she nevertheless perseveres in her attempts to fuse the borders; despite opposition from the Presbyterian minister, Shimanna continued to attend Indian ceremonials, but no water jars were broken over her grave. Like Shimanna, Ephanie lives on the margins, rejected by whites for not fulfilling their expectations of what an Indian should be, yet the Corn Dancers will not dance for her.

Even the syntax of Ephanie's speech and thought reflects her dilemma. In the novel's beginning, her speech is deliberate, labored, and non-sequential, revealing a person on the edge of a mental breakdown, a person not at home in the language of the culture. After moving to San Francisco and attending pow-wows with the pan-Indian community, her syntax becomes more logical, ordered, and purposeful, reflecting the irony of her attempt at urban Indian-ness while simultaneously trying to be white. But Ephanie doesn't belong at the Indian center anymore than she belongs at her therapy group, where she is the only non-white, requiring her to be "careful in what she said. They might think her crazy for real if she told them all of it. She knew no one would believe the tales she could tell, about the cursings, about the dyings, about the grief" (Allen, Woman 60).

Eventually the strain of double consciousness affects her mind and speech, which become disordered again as she approaches her suicide attempt. As she begins to reconcile her dual identities at the novel's conclusion, her speech and thoughts take on the mythic quality of tribal stories. The syntax reflects not just her mental state, but also her progression in the healing process. What saves her is the recognition that her mind is inviolably her own, as is her fusion of an individual and a Native consciousness into the realization that her future lies in the "Sixth World," as Grandmother Spider had intended all along. As Franz Fanon notes, "To speak, means to be in a position to use a certain syntax, to grasp the morphology of this or that language, but it means above all to assume a culture, to support the weight of a civilization" (17–18). Ephanie must endure the process by which all of the negatives of her life transform to positives: "Why it is that every going out is a coming in. Why every giving is a getting" (Allen, *Woman* 211). Her life is "the pause. The space between. The not this, not that, not the other. The place the others go around" (Allen, "Autobiography of a Confluence" 151), but it can be a place of relative harmony and balance.

Like Ephanie, Sula and Nel must come to terms with their sense of Otherness created by gender, race, class, place, spirituality, and sexuality. They are black women in an upside-down world where Bottom is top and the road to the valley is the dividing line between worlds that can be transgressed only at peril. They are black women "who had discovered years before that they were neither white nor male, and that all freedom and triumph was forbidden to them" (Morrison, *Sula* 52). In Bottom, color of skin is as crucial as it is outside of Bottom. Nel is light-skinned, while Sula is dark, but light and dark merge in them to form one child's consciousness. In Eva's words, they were "Just alike. Both of you. Never was no difference between you" (169).

Because of their communality of spirit and personhood, one would be hard put to say if the novel is Sula's or Nel's story. Both are defined to a certain extent by men: Nel by her weak husband and father, Sula by the absence of a father in a household where men are the commodity. As adults, they break with each other because of a man, Nel's husband, Jude. Nel is embedded enough in the community to assume the role of the wronged wife, thereby becoming a righteous member of the community, but Sula's individualism causes her to become an outcast, a witch whose one attempt at reconciliation with the community, her possessive love for Ajax, leads to her death. Yet, in a perverse way, Sula's actions create a stronger bond within the community at the same time that the community ostracizes her. She becomes the instrument through which the community can reaffirm its own identity and morality.

In both novels, the continuance and vitality of the oral tradition is one way by which cultural obliteration is avoided. In *Sula,* orality is more subtle and less self-conscious than in *The Woman Who Owned the Shadows,* but its presence is apparent in the narrative voice telling the stories of Plum, burned to death by his one-legged mother Eva (how she became one-legged is itself the occasion of storytelling), who is seriously burned herself trying to prevent her daughter Hannah from burning to death (and whose burning has been foretold in the dream of the red dress); of Sula, who watches with interest as her mother burns; of Shadrack, the pied-piper who leads the people of Bottom into the river on National Suicide Day. The opening lines of the novel, recalling the origins of Bottom, are cast in mythic proportions. The relationship between Sula and Nel has been foretold in their dreams. And in *Sula* there is the presence of ancestors who "are sort of timeless people whose relationships to the characters are benevolent, instructive, and protective, and they provide a certain kind of wisdom" (Morrison, "Rootedness" 343). Vashti Crutcher Lewis argues that the character of Shadrack fulfills the role of a West African water priest, who is the human embodiment of a river god. "Shadrack is the presiding river spirit for displaced African people in the Bottom" (318), who because of their cultural displacement regard him as a lunatic instead of revering him as they might in Africa. While the overt structure of the novel is linear, progressing in chronological time from 1919 to 1965, the sense of place created by the stories provides the real structure: "Maybe it hadn't been a community, but it had been a place. Now there weren't any places left, just separate houses with separate televisions and separate telephones and less and less dropping by" (Morrison, *Sula* 166). With the passing of the conditions that made storytelling a vital part of people's lives, those lives are lessened, Morrison suggests.

The presence and vitality of the oral tradition in human lives is also at the core of Allen's work. Tribal stories, legends, myths, and songs belong not just to a nostalgic cultural memory, but are integral to contemporary Native people by providing a frame of reference for dealing with problems as well as offering a sense of community in a particular past, present, and future. "The story of the people and the spirits, the story of the earth, is the story of what moves, what moves on, what patterns, what dances, what sings, what balances, so life can be felt and known. The story of life is the story of moving. Of moving on" (*Woman* 210). Like a musical composer, Allen lays out a theme in the form of a traditional story at the beginning of each of the four sections of the novel, beginning with (1) the creation of the earth and the twins, Uretsete (Iyatiku/Corn Woman) and Naotsete (Sun Woman), by Grandmother Spider; (2) the Rite of Exorcism (The Spruce Dress); (3) the friction between Naotsete and Iyatiku and the birth of the Little War Twins; and finally, (4) the reconciliation with Grandmother Spider. Variations on the major theme occur throughout each section, the most recurrent being the story of the Woman Who Fell from the Sky, whose minor theme placement belies its significance in Ephanie's developing consciousness of her identity. This story first appears in *Woman* as both a Native and a Latino myth. While the events of the story are the same in both versions, the reasons for the woman's suicide differ. In the Latino version, a woman falls in love with a man who dies in a war. Pregnant, lonely, and desperate, she climbs to the top of Picacho Peak and jumps to her death. In the Native version, the woman is

> in love with a man she was forbidden to marry. He was
> a stranger and she had fallen in love with him somehow.
> Maybe he was a Navajo. Maybe he was a Ute. But her
> love was hopeless from the start. Then the people found
> out she was seeing the youth secretly. They were very
> angry. They scolded her. Said the things that would hap-
> pen to the people because of her actions. Shamed her.
> Hurt and angry, she had gone to Picacho. (26)

While the events of the story are basically the same in both versions, they differ in motivation. In the Latino version, the woman jumps out of an individual desperation; the Native woman jumps because of the shame and misfortune her actions would bring upon the people.

The differing motivations for the suicide are significant for Ephanie. As she climbs the peak with Elena on the day that will forever alter her life, she sees and feels what the woman saw and felt on her fateful day. Ephanie becomes the legend. She continues the reenactment of the fall in other pivotal events of her life: her own unsuccessful suicide attempt and her injurious fall from the apple tree, with Stephen and Elena urging her on, the fall that altered the course of her life by fitting her into a mold of femininity and sexuality that ran counter to her true self: " 'All those years, and I never realized what had happened.' And now she knew. That what she had begun had never been completed. Because she fell she had turned her back on herself. Had misunderstood thoroughly the significance of the event. Had not even seen that she had been another sort of person before she fell. 'I abandoned myself,' she said. 'I left me' " (204).

The denial of her identity that resulted from the fall had far-reaching implications. Not only did it alter her perception of herself, but she could never again trust her own judgment, her own vision, and so tried to make other people, especially Stephen, responsible for her sanity (205).

The story of the Woman Who Fell from the Sky is also played out in the story of the young woman who marries the sorcerer and is tricked by him into falling through the hole in the ground left by the tree of light because he and the other men fear her powers. In her arrogance and innocence, she falls toward the blue light. Her free fall is broken by birds who catch her and place her amid mud on the back of Turtle, thus creating the world.

As a mixed-blood, Ephanie is a contemporary version of the Earth-diving woman, who dives "into unknown urban places now, into the racial darkness in the cities, to create a new consciousness of coexistence" (Vizenor ix). Consciousness of individualism is a relatively recent phenomenon specific to Western culture. "Through most of human history, the individual does not oppose himself to all others;

he does not feel himself to exist outside of others, and still less against others, but very much *with* others in an interdependent existence that asserts its rhythms everywhere in the community" (xix). As a mixed-blood, Ephanie's challenge is to reconcile her Western individualism within the framework of a tribal sense of community.

Flying figures also work metaphorically in *Sula.* In a grotesque turn on the African American legend of slaves who fly back to freedom in Africa, Sula and Nel trick Chicken Little up into the tree and then hurl him out into the river, where he drowns. The birds are startled by his fall, but there is no rescue as there is in the Native story, and his body is recovered from the rock and weeds by a bargeman. With their cruel childhood game turned deadly, Nel and Sula become co-conspirators. Nel worries, not that they have just killed another child, but that someone has seen. Sula, who was actually holding Chicken Little when he fell, runs to Shadrack's cabin, not to seek help but to find out if he was the shadowy figure who had watched their sacrificial offering to the river god. Like Ephanie's fall from the tree, their complicity in the death of Chicken Little is a pivotal moment for Nel and Sula, the beginning of the end of their friendship, creating "a space, a separateness between them" (64). At his funeral, while Sula cries silently and Nel worries that the finger of guilt will be pointed at her, the women of the congregation unfolded their hands "like pairs of raven's wings and flew high above their hats in the air" (65). Other images of aborted flight are associated with Ajax, Sula's lover, who leaves her to watch airplanes fly, but only from the ground, the only avenue open to a black man in his time.

Like Tommy, the spirit child, Ephanie's infant twin son who dies shortly after birth, Chicken Little is also something of a spirit child, who comes mysteriously into the narrative from the lower bank of the river and soon disappears into the water. Tommy was the secret twin, the one the doctor would not believe existed until he emerged from Ephanie's body. Like Sula and Nel's guilt over Chicken Little, Tommy's death creates much guilt for Ephanie and Thomas, who, exhausted from caring for the twins, ignore the crying babies in order to sleep, awakening in the morning to find Tommy mottled and blue, a victim of crib death. Chicken Little's body is also grotesquely disfigured, swollen and bloated by the time he is found. When Chicken Little is removed from the water, his body is dumped into a burlap sack and tossed in with the other cargo, while Tommy's body is symbolically and lovingly wrapped in the Japanese flag of the Rising Sun. At the funerals of both boys, butterflies fly over the graves.

Allen and Morrison attend closely to how natural events affect and even foretell human events. Allen says that she looks "at the natural world to see what something in the human world means" (qtd. in Crawford et al. 97). In her work, landscape is the foreground; people are the background. "We are, to me, the background upon which the land enacts *her* drama, and by landscape I don't mean only the mountains and those vast plains, but the weather, the climatic conditions and rainstorms, the overpowering thunderstorms" (97). The power of nature is primary and female in her ontology. Nature, therefore, informs her concept of femininity, which excludes such descriptives as "cute," "helpless," and "willing to be conquered": "[T]o me femininity means these great craggy mountains and these deep arroyos and tremendous storms, because mother nature after all is feminine, right?" (97). In Allen's view, human concerns and problems create the artificial aspects of the world. Nature is metaphysical, then, because part of being aware of natural phenomena is being aware of the spirits that inhabit the land along with us; Ephanie most certainly has a connection to them that sometimes is more powerful than her connectedness to what we normally call reality.

Her story begins in the quiet time of winter, the time for storytelling. The land shapes Ephanie's friendship with Elena, open and loving, until the end of the friendship, which occurs against the mythic backdrop of their climb to the top of Picacho Peak, when Elena tells Ephanie they can no longer be friends because of the developing sexual attraction between them. But even here the mountain has seen other dramas enacted upon it; as Ephanie climbs the peak, she becomes the Woman Who Fell from the Sky, and realizes that the land could have saved the woman had she been aware.

> She could have seen that, looking northward. Where the mountain called Tse'pin'a, Woman Veiled in Clouds,

waited, brooding, majestic, almost monstrously powerful. Or she could look southward, eastward, towards the
lands the people tended, that held and nurtured them. But
probably she had not looked outward. Had not seen the
sky, the piling, moving thunderheads. The gold in them.
The purpling blue. The dazzling, eye-splitting white. The
bellies of them pregnant, ripe with rain about to be born.
The living promise of their towering strength. For if she
had seen them, would she have jumped? (*Woman* 26–27)

If the woman had been connected to the land, she could have
found relief from her pain in the balance implicit in nature. The land
could not and would not have saved her without this connectedness,
because "The Mother cares for us greatly, but not for us more than
for herself" (Allen qtd. in Crawford et al. 107).

The landscape of *Sula* dominates the human activity as well. There
exists in Morrison's work a sense that human drama is not the primary
one. From the myth-like beginnings of Bottom, nature is a primary
balance in the universe, and any human attempt to alter that balance
brings repercussions.

In that place, where they tore the nightshade and the
blackberry patches from their roots to make room for the
Medallion City Golf Course, there was once a neighborhood. It stood in the hills above the valley town of Medallion and spread all the way to the river. It is called the sub-
urbs now, but when black people lived there it was called
the Bottom. One road, shaded by beeches, oaks, maples,
and chestnuts, connected it to the valley. The beeches are
gone now, and so are the pear trees where children sat
and yelled down through the blossoms to passers-by. (3)

While Morrison evades Allen's engenderment of nature as female,
a strong sense of connectedness with landscape characteristic of
Native aesthetics exists in her work. Like Allen's Shimanna (Nightshade), Morrison's nightshade is torn from its native roots to form
something new and foreign. The land has been colonized, yet the

land will eventually prevail. The connectedness of land, community, and myth is part of the African storytelling tradition upon which Morrison relies. Barbara Christian notes that

> As in the ancestral African tradition, place is as important as the human actors. For the land is a participant in the maintenance of the folk tradition. It is one of the necessary constants through which the folk dramatize the meaning of life, as it is passed on from one generation to the next. Setting then is organic to the characters' view of themselves. And a change in place dramatically alters the traditional values that give their life coherence. ("Community and Nature" 65)

Chief among these traditional values is a sense of community, but the character of Sula is frequently associated with disruptions of the natural order. Unlike the majority of the black women of Bottom, Sula has traveled outside the community. When she returns after an absence of some years, she is accompanied by a "plague of robins" whose constant dying is a harbinger of events to come and associates Sula with death. Sula's own death, which the people of Bottom thought would bring good fortune to them as though they had been cleansed of some evil in their midst, instead is followed by natural catastrophe and a renewed meanness of spirit, since with Sula dead they no longer need to be kind to each other.

The interrelationship of myth, community, and landscape reaches its fruition in the relationships between the principal female characters in *The Woman Who Owned the Shadows* and *Sula*. At the heart of both novels is the vision quest of Ephanie and Sula and Nel to ground themselves as individuals within a tribal and community context that does not completely inscribe them. As a mixed-blood, a shaman, a woman, and a lesbian, Ephanie can never be a completely tribal person, but she can arrive at a fusion of Native and Euro-American cultures that provides her with a relative sense of peace. She is able to shed her mask of passivity and recognize that she cannot depend on men to give her definition and reality. She sees as well that her most crucial relationships are those she has with women, from Elena of her childhood to Teresa of her adult years. These female relationships encompass not just childhood and adulthood but also connect her to the mythic women of her tribal past. Tradition empowers, Allen suggests, but the return to tradition is more difficult for those like Ephanie who cannot meet traditional criteria of kinship and sexuality.

Like Ephanie, Sula and Nel must come to a similar recognition that their relationship with each other is the primary one of their lives, superseding their relationships with men. Like Ephanie's second husband, Thomas, a Nisei man who really seeks a mother in a wife, Nel's husband Jude is seeking a mother in their marriage. Many other similarities exist between the male spouses in both books, including their emotional aloofness and disappointments in life. Thomas is embittered by the treatment of Japanese Americans during World War II, while Jude seethes over the emasculation of black men in this country. Given the expectations Nel and Ephanie have of men, to define and secure them, Jude's and Thomas's failure is a foregone conclusion.

Ephanie, Nel, and Sula are really seeking in their sexual relationships with men the sense of unity and completion they knew in their childhood relationships with other females. Ephanie and Elena were forced by the nun and Elena's mother to end their friendship because of the developing "taint" of homosexuality. Their breakup occurs against the phallic backdrop of the mountain. Likewise, in Sula, the pivotal moment between the girls, the drowning of Chicken Little, occurs just after the eroticism of their play in the dirt. Heterosexual society views sexuality among females as subversive, and such sexual deviation must be punished. It is permissible for Eva to incinerate Plum for the eroticism of his attempt to return to her womb, but she must be punished by her failure to save Hannah from burning to death.

While female relationships are primary in the lives of women, not all of the relationships are positive. Women punish other women for this intimacy, Allen and Morrison suggest. Most of Ephanie's contemporary (as opposed to mythic) relationships with women are hurtful. With the exception of her sometimes rocky relationship with Teresa, Ephanie's relationships with other women are negative: Teresa's Colorado friends, the nun at the hospital after Tommy dies, the women who are quick to assess responsibility for his death. Female relationships in *Sula* are equally complex: Nel's cold mother anxious to leave behind her Creole brothel roots; Hannah, who tells neighbors that she loves Sula but does not like her; Sula, who watches her mother burn to death with detached interest; Sula's abandonment of Eva after tricking her out of her money; Sula's lying to Nel about Eva's mental condition; Sula's affair with Jude; and Eva's final cursing of the upstanding Nel. Women's relationships with each other are the primary ones of their lives, but they create an intimacy and autonomy that can never be re-created in relationships with men. For example, Sula feels that she achieves perfect solitude in the sex act, while at the same time assuming an ironically submissive position that masks her subversion.

The use of the African American and Native American oral traditions in these novels suggests a commonality of content, form, and function. While I am not implying that the oral traditions are essentially the same, Leslie Marmon Silko's novel *Almanac of the Dead* explores the common link of oppression and expression that exists historically between African Americans and Native Americans in the chapter titled "One World, Many Tribes." She also chronicles the instances between 1526 and 1862 when Natives and slaves joined forces in rebellion against their mutual oppressor. bell hooks's collection of essays *Black Looks: Race and Representation* also discusses commonalities between Africans and Natives: "a reverence for nature, for life, for ancestors" (180) that contradicts the insistence of white colonialism that conflict and opposition create the natural paradigm for intercultural contact. Morrison's later novel *Beloved* shows how a Cherokee woman initiated the rescue of the fugitive slaves. Trinh T. Minh-ha points out the bind and the opportunity of those with a hyphenated identity ("Not You/Like You" 76), such as African Americans and Native Americans, whose identity is shaped in part by the oral tradition.

While Allen's use of the oral tradition is much more stylized and formal than Morrison's, perhaps reflecting a more scholarly approach to orality, both writers concern themselves with the question of how the tradition is transmitted today. For both writers, the oral tradition is not a relic, but something vital, ongoing, and essential to an individual and communal identity. In Gerald Vizenor's phrase, the myths "are not time bound, the creation takes place in the telling, in present tense metaphors" (xii). One reason Ephanie is careful to point out that she mixes her metaphors with care is because they are the tradition, and it is alive.

The oral tradition is usually presented through an elder or ancestor, but for those living in contemporary Indian and black communities, especially urban ones, close proximity to someone who knows and tells the stories may belong to a simpler past. Allen's work suggests that the myth itself functions as the ancestor, but the problem of transmission remains. Morrison sees the novel assuming the role of the Ancestor. "We don't live in places where we can hear those stories anymore; parents don't sit around and tell their children those classical, mythological archetypal stories that we had years ago" ("Rootedness" 340). Even so, Morrison acknowledges, some of the stories are too painful to be (re)membered easily, stories of the Middle Passage and slavery. Her *Beloved* is drawn from the horrifying real-life story of Margaret Garner, a fugitive slave who preferred trying to kill herself and her children rather than be returned to their owner. And, as Barbara Christian argues, even though Morrison's novels, from *The Bluest Eye* to *Song of Solomon,* move progressively deeper into history, Solomon's flight back to Africa is blocked by the immutable reality of the Middle Passage ("Fixing Methodologies" 12).

Running through the epilogue to *Beloved* is the refrain, "It was not a story to pass on." Yet, in order to reclaim their history, in order to reclaim themselves, African Americans must remember the Middle Passage in all its genocidal ugliness because, as Christian asserts, it is "the dividing line between being African and being African American," a four-hundred-year holocaust that "has practically disappeared from American cultural memory" (7). In conjuring the ghostly Beloved, Morrison narrates the story of the lost "Sixty Million and more" to whom the novel is dedicated. The painful stories and the ancient stories and their modern reenactments have to be told in some way; the novel provides an ideal forum because of its affective and participatory qualities. Like the oral tradition, the novel demands the audience's participation as the writer and the reader together create the ceremony of meaning. At the conclusion of her latest novel, *Jazz*, Morrison makes explicit the interaction between text and reader, and the reader's role in creating meaning. In the monologue that concludes the book, the narrative voice addresses the reader directly: "If I were able I'd say it. Say make me, remake me. You are free to do it and I am free to let you because look, look. Look where your hands are. Now" (229), as the reader's hands are positioned holding open the pages of the book.

The focus on female relationships that prevails in both novels suggests that gender is aligned with orality and place as agents of cultural affirmation and transformation. Both novels are in a very real sense female vision quests in which the vision sought is identification and reconciliation of an individual and communal consciousness. For Ephanie, Sula, and Nel, that reconciliation can occur only within their female relationships, in specific landscapes, through the power of storytelling. By drawing upon the oral roots of their respective cultures, Allen and Morrison not only preserve that aspect of their cultures, but also transform it to demonstrate that the past and the present, as well as orality and literacy, are vital parts of the same continuous cultural process of coming to voice.

6

DARK CONTINENT / DARK WOMAN

Hélène Cixous and Joy Harjo

For each of us as women, there is a dark place within, where hidden and growing our true spirit rises, "beautiful / and tough as chestnut / stanchions against (y)our nightmare of weakness/" and of impotence.
                    —Audre Lorde, "Poetry Is Not a Luxury"

And so, in times of strangeness, by sharing unhappiness, by being strangers together, people and poet constitute an internal homeland.
                    —Hélène Cixous, "We Who Are Free"

If I am a poet who is charged with speaking the truth (and I believe the word poet is synonymous with truth-teller), what do I have to say about all of this?
                    —Joy Harjo,
        "A Postcolonial Tale," The Woman Who Fell from the Sky

Reflecting on the pervasive but unnamed Africanist presence in canonical American literature, Toni Morrison, in her trilogy of essays *Playing in the Dark: Whiteness and the Literary Imagination,* notes the contradictory nature of mainstream writers' obsession with color: "Images of blackness can be evil *and* protective, rebellious *and* forgiving, fearful *and* desirable—all of the self-contradictory images of the self. Whiteness, alone, is mute, meaningless, unfathomable, pointless, frozen, veiled, curtained, dreaded, senseless, implacable. Or so our writers seem to say" (59). Morrison goes on to argue, in a chapter appropriately titled "Romancing the Shadow," that the self-reflexive shadow cast throughout American literary history almost certainly is the African shadow that merges into the deeper shadow of the presumed " 'raw, half-savage world' " that constitutes the American natural and psychic landscape. Morrison allows the *possibility* that the indigenous people of the Americas are the source of this motivating loss of light in the wilderness, but then dismisses it. "Why is it seen as raw and savage? Because it is peopled by a non-white indigenous population? Perhaps. But certainly because there is ready to hand a bound and unfree, rebellious but serviceable, black population against which . . . all white men are enabled to measure these privileging and privileged differences" (45).

Morrison's dismissal of the privileging power of the indigenous dark presence is especially curious in light of the fact that in *Beloved* it is a fugitive band of the sick Cherokee that shelters Paul D and the other escapees from the slave chain gang. A Cherokee woman begins the rescue process by bravely initiating contact with the slaves, and the other Cherokee feed the black men from a pot of mush while hacking away at their chains, all the while telling stories in the misty darkness of the forest (112). Symbolically and literally, the Cherokee free the blacks from bondage and then point the way toward more lasting freedom in the North, with the slightly stereotypical exhortation of the mystical/close-to-nature Indian to "Follow the tree flowers . . . Only the tree flowers. As they go, you go. You will be where you want to be when they are gone" (112).

One of the most striking aspects of *Beloved* is the sense of unity those starving Cherokee obviously feel with another displaced and betrayed dark people. Morrison captures simply and eloquently the common link of oppression, the same link that Leslie Marmon Silko explores in *Almanac of the Dead* as she chronicles the numerous instances in which slaves and Native Americans combined forces against their mutual oppressors. Yet Morrison's essay "Romancing the Shadow," the middle essay of the collection, repudiates that link by establishing not a commonality but a polarity and hierarchy of oppressions. This polarity becomes even more curious as Morrison uses the darkness of Indians as metaphor for racial subservience and female self-loathing. In the third essay in the trilogy, "Disturbing Nurses and the Kindness of Sharks," her discussion of Hemingway's *The Garden of Eden* describes the male Africans who serve the Hemingway hero as "Tontos all, whose role is to do everything possible to serve the Lone Ranger" (*Playing in the Dark* 82), and Catherine Bourne's obsession with tanning her pale skin under the African sun, because " 'I want every part of me dark and it's getting that way and you'll be darker than an Indian' " (86). Morrison's elision of darkness and femaleness demonstrates how deeply imbedded in Western cultural thought is this damaging association.

This same complex link between the self-reflexive nature of darkness and femaleness, the romance of the shadow, is at the heart of the work of Hélène Cixous and Joy Harjo. Both writers employ the concept of transformation articulated by philosopher Drucilla Cornell, "Change radical enough to so restructure any system—political, legal or social—that the 'identity' of the system is itself altered" (1), in order to explore the seeming paradox of reconciling their internal need for subjectivity and voice with external historical processes of division, without re-creating dualities, hierarchies, oppositions, and polarities. Implicit in Cornell's definition of transformation is consideration of the individual transformation that must occur concurrent with systemic transformation, "because we can only truly rethink performative possibility if we also confront what kind of subject could be open to the creation of new worlds" (1). As Paula Gunn Allen points out in *The Sacred Hoop,* Harjo has arrived at her view of the permeability of all boundaries from reading the work of American feminists (166), but strong congruences exist as well between Harjo's thought and the work of one of the most lyrical theorists of transformative French philosophy, Hélène Cixous. These congruences are so marked that the two writers could be engaged in an ongoing dialogue that reveals the transformative power of language to change fear and hatred, the shadowy areas of their lives, into forgiveness and healing by questioning and ultimately rejecting the polarities implicit in phallocentric culture and its discourse.

Harjo and Cixous both struggle to reconcile their sense of multiple identities that arise from the displacements of history and family background. For Harjo, of Creek/Anglo ancestry, knowledge of her tribal history gives rise to a tribal consciousness of the disastrous effects on her cultural and individual identity of a forced removal from ancestral land, for a sense of place is crucial to a sense of self. As she writes in the preface to *Secrets from the Center of the World,*

> All landscapes have a history, much the same as people exist within cultures, even tribes. There are distinct voices, languages that belong to particular areas. There are voices inside rocks, shallow washes, shifting skies; they are not silent. And there is movement, not always the violent motion of earthquakes associated with the earth's motion or the steady unseen swirl through the heavens, but other motion, subtle, unseen, like breathing. A motion, a sound, that if you allow your own inner workings to stop long enough, moves into the place inside you that mirrors a similar landscape; you too can see it, feel it, hear it, know it.

But when one's tribal memory encompasses a silencing of the intimate voice of place, and a genocidal march from Alabama to Oklahoma becomes the only certain motion, how does one for whom memory is alive survive with the knowledge of what has been lost, of what is to come? Gloria Anzaldúa observes that "the dark-skinned woman has been silenced, gagged, caged, bound into servitude with marriage, bludgeoned for three hundred years, sterilized and castrated in the twentieth century" (*Borderlands/La Frontera* 22), and she copes by developing a "tolerance for contradictions, a tolerance for ambiguities" (79). Harjo acknowledges as much when she says, "living is like a diamond or how they cut really fine stones. There are not just two sides but there are so many and they all make up a whole" (qtd. in Bruchac 95). For Harjo, the multifaceted complexity of her life prevents her from returning to the simplicity of tribal roots because her roots are not wholly tribal, not wholly Oklahoma. It is "a different place, a mythical place. It's a spiritual landscape that Oklahoma is part of—I always see Oklahoma as my mother, my motherland. . . . but my return usually takes place on a mythical level. . . . it's one of my homes" (qtd. in Coltelli 56–57).

Harjo has experienced all the negative aspects of being a contemporary mixed-blood person. "I come from a dispossessed people," she told the "Poetics and Politics" seminar at the University of Arizona. Dispossession encompasses the personal and the tribal, the linguistic and the aesthetic. Harjo speaks of the brutality of her "own border status" ("Poetics and Politics" 9) in her poem "Autobiography," which relates how her father "searched out his death with the vengeance of a warrior who has been the hunted," and how "Even at two I knew we were different. Could see through the eyes of strangers that we were trespassers in the promised land." Her mother's attempts to instill a personal and cultural pride through storytelling resulted only in a sense of confusion arising from a bifurcated vision of self. "At five I was designated to string beads in kindergarten. At seven I knew how to play chicken and win. And at fourteen I was drinking" (*In Mad Love and War* 14). As she acknowledges to Bruchac, she has "gone through the stage where I hated everybody who wasn't Indian, which meant part of myself. I went through a really violent kind of stage with that" (*Survival This Way* 95). She acknowledges as well that a sense of dispossession sometimes estranges her from the "community" of other Native writers, which would seem to be her natural home. But she also speaks of her need to leave "home," and of the pain involved in separating from her "psychic support." At a writer's forum composed of herself, Simon Ortiz, Leslie Marmon Silko, Pablita Vailliarte, Lawrence Vaillo, and Joe Sando, Harjo realized that she was the only non-Pueblo writer on the panel and how her particular tribal history distinguishes her writing from that of the other writers, "Because I realized that my experience is totally different. Yes, my tribe has the same kinds of themes in place inherently. But we have a very different history. And my history within the structure of that tribe is still very different" ("Poetics and Politics" 9).

The estrangement from self and community—and the resulting self-destructiveness of the mixed-blood person—is rooted partially in alienation from her native language. As a woman and a writer, Harjo must find her voice in the language of the patriarchal colonizer, a precarious negotiation at best. As Laura Coltelli points out, in Native cultures "Words . . . are not mere referents, they are life-giving" (2). When the essence of language is creativity, how does a writer give life to ideas in a medium of death, duplicity, and destruction, which the English language has been for Native people? Even now, Harjo still struggles to find her voice.

> I still have a sense of not being able to say things well. I think much of the problem is with the English language; it's a very materialistic and a very subject-oriented language. I don't know Creek, but I know a few words and I am familiar with tribal languages more so than I am my own. What I've noticed is that the center of tribal languages often has nothing to do with things, objects, but contains a more spiritual sense of the world. Maybe that's why I write poetry, because it's one way I can speak. Writing poetry enables me to speak of things that are more difficult to speak of in "normal" conversations. (qtd. in Bruchac 94)

Poetry, then, becomes the means to overcome the materialism of English; poetry "becomes the way to speak the sacred," a way to transmit to her audience "the myth inside themselves" ("Poetics and Politics" 19). Her poem "Resurrection"—for the violence-torn and music-filled Nicaraguan border town of Esteli, whose incongruent sounds of gunfire and love songs prophesies the coming of "a language so terrible / it could resurrect us all" (*In Mad Love and War* 18)—speaks to the power of poetry to heal the violent divisions of her own soul. Her mixed-blood status is a burden she did not seek, yet she has also arrived at the point where she can view it fatalistically as a responsibility and an opportunity: "I don't believe there are any accidents in why people were born where they were, or are. There are no accidents. So I realize that being born an American Indian woman in this time and place is with a certain reason, a certain purpose. There are seeds of dreams I hold, and responsibility, that go with being born someone, especially a woman of my tribe, who is also a part of this invading other culture, and the larger globe" (qtd. in Coltelli 60). She has reached the point in her life where she finds her strength by giving voice to the conflicting ambiguities and negotiations that have been placed before her:

. . . you can approach anything and use it; it's like fire, you know, there are always ways to work within something. . . . I suppose in this country and day and age and time and being a woman and everything else that I've learned to use conflict; either I've had to or I wouldn't have been alive. I almost died when I was in my late teens . . . you know, suicide, etc. . . . because I was using those things against me, those conflicts had turned against me and were chasing me down; it's like at some point you take them and you use those. At some point, and I think that's what maybe writing and other writers and other human beings in my life that have taught me is that conflict can be rich and invaluable. ("Poetics and Politics" 25)

In translating the conflicts of her life into the rhythms of poetry, Harjo finds a sense of humor to be a necessity. As she told the "Poetics and Politics" seminar, the stories she is currently writing are funny. "I wish I could write comedy. That's one of my secret goals is to write comedy. That's been the point is here's the incredible conflict and you make something. There is some beauty in it. There is a point of beauty in it, as well as the humor" (25).

That she finds humor to be a vital component of her work comes as something of a surprise, given the customary seriousness of her subject matter—a metaphysics made personal and tangible—and her graceful language. But on closer examination, a darkly tinged, fatalistic humor subtly weaves its way through some of her most apparently serious work. "Deer Dancer," the opening poem of the generally somber collection *In Mad Love and War,* contains several examples of humor in the midst of pathos. "We were the Indian ruins. / She was the end of beauty" is Harjo's description of the woman who danced naked for the "hardcore" bar patrons on the coldest night of winter, a woman so beautiful that even Henry Jack, "who could not survive a sober day, thought she was Buffalo Calf Woman come back, passed out, his head near the toilet. All night he dreamed a dream he could not say. The next day he borrowed money, went home, and sent back the money I lent. Now that's a miracle. Some people see vision in a burned tortilla, some in the face of a woman." A compassionate humor is also present in the pithy description of Richard's jealous wife, who must be restrained from making weapons of the contents of her pockets—knives and diaper pins; and in Harjo's sardonic response to the ultimate pick-up/put-down line: " 'What's a girl like you doing in a place like this?' / That's what I'd like to know, what are we all doing in a place like this?" as the jukebox plays a universally recognized song of loss: " 'You picked a fine time to leave me, Lucille. / With four hungry children and a crop in the field.' " (6).

The humor in Harjo's poetry is always underscored by a sense of multiple worlds and a recognition of the tenuousness of human endeavors in the scheme of mythic time. Just as the beautiful woman dancing naked in the bar "was the myth slipped down through dreamtime" (6), still vitally evocative in the midst of indignity, so also is the slippage between chronological and mythic time made visible through the derisive wisdom of "that fool crow, picking through trash near the corral," who "understands the center of the world as greasy scraps of fat. Just ask him. He doesn't have to say that the earth has turned scarlet through fierce belief, after centuries of heartbreak and laughter—he perches on the blue bowl of the sky, and laughs" (*Secrets from the Center of the World* 2).

As Harjo's use of it reveals, humor is a point of power and transition into the natural/mythic world from the artificial/chronological world, breaking down boundaries, and obscuring borders, because we recognize ourselves sitting in the bar, voyeurs to the woman's dance, and know that Crow's laughter is finally directed at us. And it is through the natural world that mythic time finds its voice, if we but listen for it. In "Javelina," Harjo writes, "The mythic world will enter with the subtlety of a snake the color of earth changing skin," as she juxtaposes the temporal "soap opera" of the seventeen-year-old girl, her baby, and husband outside the cheap motel in South Tucson, with the timeless wisdom of the desert's natural environment: javelinas, cicadas, turtles, prickly pear, and rain (*In Mad Love and War* 31).

Recognizing one's shifting identity and place of origin in the modern world is also crucial to Hélène Cixous. As she relates in "Sorties,"

I come, biographically, from a rebellion, from a violent and anguished direct refusal to accept what is happening on the stage on whose edge I find I am placed, as a result of the combined accidents of History. I had this strange 'luck': a couple of rolls of the dice, a meeting between two trajectories of the diaspora, and at the end of these roots of expulsion and dispersion that mark the functioning of western History through the displacements of Jews, I fall. (70)

Born in colonized Algeria to displaced Jewish parents, their father Sephardic and their mother Ashkenazy, her brothers, by virtue of having been born in exile, are Arabs. Cixous struggles to reconcile her multiple and conflicting identities:

Who am I? I am 'doing' French history. I am a Jewish woman. In which ghetto was I penned up during your wars and your revolutions? . . . . What is my name? . . . Who is this 'I'? Where is my place? I am looking. I search everywhere. I read, I ask. I begin to speak. Which language is mine? French? German? Arabic? Who spoke for me throughout the generations? It's my luck. What an accident! Being born in Algeria, not in France, not in Germany; a little earlier and, like some members of my family, I would not be writing today. I would anonymiserate eternally from Auschwitz. ("Sorties" 71).

Like Harjo, Cixous was made aware from a very early age of her special border status. Because her father was a military doctor during World War II, the family had use of the Officers' Club in Oran, which she describes as a garden oasis in the midst of the desert. It was here, at the age of three, that she first encountered anti-Semitism, when other children attacked her before she was old enough to comprehend that the boundaries of religion superseded the privileges of class (Suleiman xix). Her language became, like her religion, another reinforcement of her border status. The language of her home was German, which she learned as her language of play, but in school it became a language of intolerable restrictions. She also learned English, French, Hebrew, and Arabic, but has not felt entirely at home in any of them because she believes she has "no legitimate place, no land, no fatherland, no history of my own" (*"Coming to Writing"* 15). Her sense of the hierarchy underlying all human relationships under colonialism was reinforced by her early observations of Oran street life.

> So I am three or four years old and the first thing I see in the street is that the world is divided in half, organized hierarchically, and that it maintains this distribution through violence. I see that there are those who beg, who die of hunger, misery, and despair, and that there are offenders who die of wealth and pride, who stuff themselves, who crush and humiliate. Who kill. And who walk around in a stolen country as if they had the eyes of their souls put out. Without seeing that others are alive. (70)

With such a negative inventory facing her, she eventually comes to the realization that "At a certain moment for the person who has lost everything, whether that means a being or a country, language becomes the country. One enters the country of words" (qtd. in Suleiman xx). Yet even the country of words as found in writing was not the refuge she initially sought. Even though she believed that "writing is not obliged to reproduce the system" (*"Coming to Writing"* 72), what she found in books was struggle and cultural stereotypes of female passivity or, conversely, perverse female power: "What is my place if I am a woman? I look for myself throughout the centuries and don't see myself anywhere. I know now that my fighters are masculine and that their value almost inevitably is limited: they are great in the eyes of men and for each other. But only on the condition that a woman not appear and make blind and grotesque tyrants of them" (75).

The country of language to which women are relegated in Western thought is the cultural mythology of the Joycean "Bridebed, childbed, bed of death" ("Sorties" 66). Like Harjo's tribal mythology, Western cultural myth is ever-present in the mantra-like "Once upon a time . . . once . . . and once again" (66), but unlike the cultural empowerment of women in Harjo's tribal mythology, Cixous's culture reinforces the belief that "Either woman is passive or she does not exist" (64): "Beauties slept in their woods, waiting for princes to come and wake them up. In their beds, in their glass coffins, in their childhood forests like dead women. Beautiful, but passive; hence desirable: all mystery emanates from them. It is men who like to play dolls. As we have known since Pygmalion" (66).

The phallogocentric nature of written language compels Cixous to experiment with structures and forms in order to "write past the wall." Just as Harjo complains of the materialistic and objective nature of English, of its lack of a spiritual center, so also Cixous tries to return writing to the body, to open it up to structures that are nonhierarchical and nonexclusive of sexuality—a narrative form employing multiple and shifting subjectivities. Such feminine language is playful and ironic, embodied in poetry and song because of their proximity to the subconscious mind. Producing it is a liberating act, one that permits the "newly born woman" to fly/steal. Cixous argues that women must "steal what they need from the dominant culture, but then fly away with their cultural booty to the 'in-between', where new images, new narratives, and new subjectivities can be created" (qtd. in Shiach 23).

Coming from displaced peoples—accidents of history to Cixous, the fulfillment of fate to Harjo—both writers are painfully aware that they are survivors, "a stolen people in a stolen land" (Harjo, *In Mad Love and War* 14), but the strength of the survivor is reflected in their work. In her poem "Anchorage," Harjo finds that renewal in the Athabascan grandmother curled up on the park bench, "smelling like 200 years / of blood and piss." In the story of the homeless grandmother is contained "the fantastic and terrible story of all of our survival / those who were never meant / to survive" (*She Had Some Horses* 14–15). Harjo explains, "And it's like a big joke that any of us are here because they tried so hard to make sure we weren't, you know, either kill our spirits, move us from one place to another, try to take our minds and to take our hearts" (qtd. in Bruchac 90). Similarly, it is through language, Cixous argues in her Amnesty lecture, that we are able to continue: "when we are led into the never-again and the nowhere that lie behind the barbed wire, *a native land remains to us:*

language, a land that *moves with us,* a land that is its own salvation" ("We Who Are Free" 209).

In "Reflections on Exile," Edward Said writes of the conflicts of the exile as trope for the conflicts of the twentieth century, with its totalitarian regimes, wars, famines, and political injustices. He views the history of this century as a struggle between two opposite poles of the political axis: nationalism and exile, with exile being the "unhealable rift forced between a human being and a native place, between the self and its true home" (357).

While Said and other post-colonial theorists resolutely overlook the dislocation of indigenous peoples that began in the Western hemisphere in the fifteenth century, much of what he says about nationalism and exile holds true for Harjo and Cixous. Exile is both a burden and an opportunity because "homes are always provisional. Borders and barriers, which enclose us within the safety of a familiar territory, can also become prisons, and are often defended beyond reason or necessity. Exiles cross borders, break barriers of thought and experience" (Said, "Reflections on Exile" 365).

A sense of shifting identities and places of origin is the result of these displacements and may be the key to survival in the contemporary world for the mixed-blood woman. Cixous believes that "All poets know that the self is in permanent mutation, that it is not one's own, that it is always in movement, in a trance, astray, and that it goes out towards you. That is the free self. Our time is afraid of losing and afraid of losing itself. But one can write *only* by losing oneself, by going astray, just as one can love only at the risk of losing oneself and of losing" ("We Who Are Free" 203).

Throughout the constant negotiations of their lives, a hallmark of the work of Cixous and Harjo is its strong woman-identification. Harjo has said that "the word 'feminism' doesn't carry over to the tribal world, but a concept mirroring similar meanings would" (qtd. in Coltelli 60). That concept she names "empowerment." Because she sees no contradiction between femininity and strength, the women of Harjo's poetry are warriors. In her discussion with Helen Jaskoski, she says,

I believe those so-called "womanly" traits are traits of the warrior. Vulnerability is one, you know. The word, warrior, it applies to women just as well. I don't see it as exclusive to a male society. Male and female traits are within each human, anyway. They've stood up in the face of danger, in the face of hopelessness. They've been brave—not in the national headlines, but they've been true to themselves, and who they are, and to their families. Their act of bravery could have been to feed their children, to more than survive. ("A MELUS Interview" 11)

They are women warriors such as Jacqueline Peters, whose 1986 lynching in Lafayette, California, by the Ku Klux Klan is marked in Harjo's poem "Strange Fruit." The voice of the poem becomes Peters's voice affirming her personal and cultural innocence: "I didn't do anything wrong. I did not steal from your mother. My brother did not take your wife. I did not break into your home, tell you how to live or die. Please. Go away, hooded ghosts from hell on earth. I only want heaven in my baby's arms, my baby's arms" (*In Mad Love and War* 11–12). The poem juxtaposes images of light and darkness to demonstrate the sometimes contradictory meanings of the metaphors. White is the color of the moon and the safety of the lamp burning in her house, but it is also the robes of the KKK and the illumination that permits her no hiding place. The images of motion, represented in her dancing feet, which "have known where to take me, to where the sweet things grow," are also the feet that "betray me, dance anyway from this killing tree" (12).

Jacqueline Peters's "crime" was attempting to organize a chapter of the NAACP following the lynching of a black man. Other warriors are the women of Nicaragua whose torturers speak American English, and Anna Mae Aquash, an AIM activist at Pine Ridge in 1976, who was shot in the back of the head at close range, her body later mutilated by the FBI.

These warrior women fight political battles, and personal ones as well. They are the seventeen-year-old girl with the baby on her hip, of the poem "Javelina," standing at the pay phone in South Tucson, a nameless girl in whom Harjo sees the reflection of her own young womanhood. "Do I need a job? Has the car broken down again? Does the license plate say Oklahoma?" (*In Mad Love and War* 31). Harjo would like to stop, to give the girl/herself the benefit of the wisdom gained through her years of hard experience: that she is connected to a timelessness. "The mythic world will enter with the subtlety of a snake the color of the earth changing skin. Your wounded spirit is the chrysalis for a renascent butterfly. Your son will graduate from high school. You have a daughter not yet born, and you who thought you could say nothing, write poetry" (*In Mad Love and War* 31). These stories of warrior women would go unremembered if Harjo did not keep them alive in her own story, "for we remember the story and must tell it again so we may all live" (7).

Remembering and retelling these stories necessarily invokes anger, but Harjo sees the potential of women's anger to produce positive results. For example, in "For Anna Mae Pictou Aquash . . ." the murdered woman's story comes to Harjo through the women's storytelling. Women's anger, Harjo suggests, is a powerfully creative force. To Bruchac, she quotes a favorite line by Gandhi: "I have learned through bitter experience the one supreme lesson to conserve my anger, and as heat conserved is transmitted into energy, even so our anger, controlled, can be transmitted into power which can move the world" (96). Harjo finds a parallel among colonial oppressions that serves as an exemplary story of negation transformed to affirmation. "It seems that the Native American experience has often been bitter. Horrible things have happened over and over. I like to think that bitter experience can be used to move the world, and if we can see that and work toward that instead of killing each other and hurting each other through all the ways that we have done it" (qtd. in Bruchac 96).

Cixous, too, believes women to be warriors whose poetry transforms the abuses of power. In her Amnesty lecture she writes, "For years, I wondered whether poetry would hold up in the concentration camps, if the tongue would not shrivel, if the magic weapon would not dissolve into dust. Till the day when I met women resistance fighters who gave me the answer: in periods of spiritual penury, human beings need books, need you, need to address you, need an extra voice" ("We Who Are Free" 208).

Women's anger, expressed through the supremely political act of writing, undermines patriarchy's impulse to categorize, polarize, hierarchize, and dualize, by interrogating opposition as the organizing principle of Western discourse. Cixous's famous passage in "Sorties" asks,

> Where is she?
> Activity/passivity
> Sun/moon
> Culture/nature
> Day/night
> Father/mother
> Head/heart
> Intelligent/palpable
> Logos/pathos
> Form, convex, step, advance, semen, progress
> Matter, concave, ground—where steps are taken, holding- and dumping-ground.
> Man
> ———
> Woman
>
> (63)

In these oppositions, the female is always the less valorized, the trivialized, as if the rule of law is a natural, and not a cultural, imposition. Always she moves within *his* universe, the outsider, the Other, the shadow who views herself through *his* gaze. She is the "dark continent," who is "taught her name, that hers is the dark region: because you are Africa, you are black. Your continent is dark. Dark is dangerous. You can't see anything in the dark, you are afraid. Don't move, you might fall. Above all don't go into the forest" ("Sorties" 68).

Darkness, in other words, is fearful; darkness is female. The most damaging aspect of this metaphor is its reflexivity. Women who are taught by their culture to view themselves through the male gaze find that their greatest fear is the fear of themselves. "And we have internalized this fear of the dark. Women haven't had eyes for themselves. They haven't gone exploring in their house. Their sex still frightens them. Their bodies, which they haven't dared enjoy, have been colonized. Woman is disgusted by woman and fears her" ("Sorties" 68).

Such a system of oppositional duality is itself a form of gendered colonialism, a parallel to nationalistic colonialism. Nationalistic difference, like gendered difference, under this paradigm of power, depends on the subservience of one element to the other: woman to man, Algeria to France, indigenous to colonist, Africa to Europe. The Other not only is inferior, it must also be repressed because, despite its inferiority, and because of its inevitability, danger resides in its darkness and its femaleness.

This culturally imposed self-fear and self-loathing have haunted Harjo's poetry through the metaphor of horses. In "Ice Horses," she writes: "These are the ones who escape / after the last hurt is turned inward / they are the dangerous ones" (*She Had Some Horses* 67). In "I Give You Back," she confronts her internalization of hundreds of years of cultural and sexual oppression:

> Oh you have choked me, but I gave you the leash.
> You have gutted me, but I gave you the knife.
> You have devoured me, but I lay myself across the fire.
> You held my mother down and raped her,
> but I gave you the heated thing.
> (She Had Some Horses 74)

For Harjo, the recognition of the source of her fear is the first step toward overcoming it. "She had some horses she loved. / She had some horses she hated. / These were the same horses" (64). From the recognition comes the strength to confront fear, "her beloved and hated twin" (73), and relinquish it. Yet, as she acknowledges, the act of releasing her fear carries with it the tender realization that she is losing an essential part of herself.

Reclaiming agency and language from patriarchal culture and its imperialistic polarities through their writing begins the process of healing for Harjo and Cixous. Cixous writes,

The "Dark Continent" is neither dark nor unexplorable: It is still unexplored only because we have been made to believe that it was too dark to be explored. Because they want to make us believe that what interests us is the white continent, with its monument to Lack. And we believed. We have been frozen in our place between two terrifying myths: between the Medusa and the Abyss. . . . All you have to do to see the Medusa is look her in the face: and she isn't deadly. She is beautiful and she laughs. ("Sorties" 68–69)

For Harjo, as well, the transformation comes when women address the pernicious effects of Western cultural myths of gender and ethnicity under which they have been forced to operate, an "abyss" of history that keeps them only half alive because so many things are left unspoken. Based on a genocidal history in which "there are more bones of native peoples, of indigenous peoples, in museums in this country than there are living people" ("Poetics and Politics" 73), she argues that Native women's writing, such as Leslie Marmon Silko's *Almanac of the Dead,* forces writers to confront the abyss and walk through it, a terrifying process of speaking the silence.

But what happens if we talk about it? It's going to be terrifying. But what the hell, I'd rather be alive and walk through it terrified than to sit around anymore and just keep my mouth shut about it. This country is stunted until everyone, in their own way, addresses that abyss in their own way and walks through it. . . . This has to do with everybody in this country, not just Indian people. It has to do with everyone, just as this abyss. It's not just our loss, it's the loss of everyone in this country. And that's what has to be walked through in some way. ("Poetics and Politics" 73)

When the transformation comes, it will come with the force of anger so powerful that it will transform the world, just as Gandhi predicted, except that this transformation will occur as the result of *women's* anger. And it is this same gendered creative power that Cixous and Harjo articulate with uncanny similarity. In Cixous's words:

> When "The Repressed" of their culture and their society come back, it is an explosive return, which is *absolutely* shattering, staggering, overturning, with a force never let loose before, on the scale of the most tremendous repressions: for at the end of the Age of the Phallus, women will have been either wiped out or heated to the highest, most violent, white-hot fire. Throughout their deafening, dumb history, they have lived in dreams, embodied but still deadly silent, in silences, in voiceless rebellions. ("Sorties" 95)

Harjo also describes the transformation in explosive terms, but in terms that relate repression to the natural world, suggesting that the repression of women's voices/bodies is intimately linked to the repression of the earth's voice/body:

> But maybe the explosion was horses,
> bursting out of the crazy earth
> near Okemah. They were a violent birth,
> . . . .
> Some will not see them.
> But some will see the horses with their hearts of sleeping
> volcanoes and will be rocked awake
> past their bodies
> to see who they have become.
> *(She Had Some Horses* 68–69)

Harjo's and Cixous's work exemplifies the difficult process of transforming self-hatred into self-love. Harjo's poem "Transformation" is a distillation of her thought on the necessity, in a so-called post-colonial world, of "writing past the wall," walls erected between people, between the divided self, between time and genre, between text and life. Exemplifying Cixous's belief that "a body is always a substance for inscription" ("Coming to Writing" 26), the poem reclaims darkness and femaleness by creating its own transformation of hatred and fear into love and forgiveness: "That's what I mean to tell you. On the other side of the place you live stands a dark woman. She has been trying to talk to you for years. You have called the same name in the middle of a nightmare, from the center of miracles. She is beautiful. This is your hatred back. She loves you" (*In Mad Love and War* 59).

In the work of Hélène Cixous and Joy Harjo, language offers the place, the country, where transformation of hate and anger into forgiveness and healing can occur. The past and its stories are continuously retold in language that (re)fuses the body to the earth. Although each must write in a language of dual colonization, of a non-native tongue in a non-feminine form, both seek a new language, a new form of expression that is radically transformative of political institutions and the individuals who will inhabit them. Through long histories of personal dislocations and exiles, Cixous and Harjo have learned that by embracing their multiple identities and places of origin, they transform and create, thereby gaining a measured healing that permits them to "more than survive."

REFERENCES

Alcoff, Linda. "Cultural Feminism versus Post-Structuralism: The Identity Crisis in Feminist Theory." *Signs: Journal of Women in Culture and Society* 13.3 (1988): 405–36.

———. "The Problem of Speaking for Others." *Cultural Critique* 0882–4371 (Winter 1991–92): 5–32.

Alilkatuktuk, Jeela. "Canada: Stranger in My Own Land." *MS* 3 (February 1974): 8–10.

Allen, Paula Gunn. "The Autobiography of a Confluence." *I Tell You Now: Autobiographical Essays by Native American Writers.* Ed. Brian Swann and Arnold Krupat. Lincoln: U of Nebraska P, 1987. 141–54.

———. " 'Border' Studies: The Intersection of Gender and Color." *Introduction to Scholarship in Modern Languages and Literature.* Ed. Joseph Gibaldi. New York: MLA, 1992. 303–17.

———. "I Climb the Mesas in My Dreams." *Survival This Way: Interviews with American Indian Poets.* Ed. Joseph Bruchac. Tucson: Sun Tracks and U of Arizona P, 1987. 1–21.

———. Interview. *This Is about Vision: Interviews with Southwestern Writers.* Ed. John F. Crawford and others. Albuquerque: U of New Mexico P, 1990. 95–107.

———. Introduction. *Spider Woman's Granddaughters: Traditional Tales and Contemporary Writing by Native American Women.* Ed. Allen. Boston: Beacon, 1989. 1–21.

———. *The Sacred Hoop: Recovering the Feminine in American Indian Traditions.* Boston: Beacon, 1986.

———. *The Woman Who Owned the Shadows.* San Francisco: Spinsters/Aunt Lute, 1983.

Anzaldúa, Gloria. *Borderlands/La Frontera: The New Mestiza.* San Francisco: Spinsters/Aunt Lute, 1987.

————, ed. "Haciendo caras, una entrada." *Making Face, Making Soul: Creative and Critical Perspectives by Women of Color.* San Francisco: Aunt Lute, 1990. xv–xxvii.

Armstrong, Jeanette. *Slash.* Penticon, B.C.: Theytus, 1985.

Babcock, Barbara. "At Home, No Womens Are Storytellers: Potteries, Stories, and Politics in Cochiti Pueblo." *Journal of the Southwest* 30.3 (Autumn 1988): 356–89.

————. "The Story in the Story: Metanarration in Folk Narrative." *Verbal Art as Performance.* Ed. Richard Bauman. Prospect Heights, IL: Waveland, 1977. 61–79.

————. "Taking Liberties, Writing from the Margins, and Doing It with a Difference." *Journal of American Folklore* 100.398 (October-December 1987): 390–411.

Backerman, Jane. "The Seams Can't Show: An Interview with Toni Morrison." *Black American Literature Forum* 12.1 (Spring 1978): 56–60.

Bakhtin, Mikhail M. *The Dialogic Imagination.* Trans. Caryl Emerson and Michael Holquist. Ed. Michael Holquist. Austin: U of Texas P, 1981.

Barnett, Don. Introduction. *Bobbi Lee, Indian Rebel: Struggles of a Native Canadian Woman.* By Lee Maracle. Ed. Barnett.

Basso, Keith H. " 'Speaking with Names': Language and Landscape among the Western Apache." *Cultural Anthropology* 3.2 (May 1988): 99–130.

Bataille, Gretchen, and Kathleen Mullen Sands. *American Indian Women: Telling Their Lives.* Linclon: U of Nebraska P, 1984.

Bauer, Dale M., and S. Jaret McKinstry, eds. *Feminism, Bakhtin, and the Dialogic.* Albany: State U of New York P, 1991.

Bauman, Richard. *Story, Performance, Event: Contextual Studies of Oral Narrative.* Bloomington: Indiana UP, 1990.

Behar, Ruth. Introduction. "Women Writing Culture: Another Telling of the Story of American Anthropology." *Critique of Anthropology* 13.4 (1993): 307–25.

Berkhofer, Robert F. *The White Man's Indian: Images of the American Indian from Columbus to the Present.* New York: Vintage, 1978.

Bevis, William. "Native American Novels: Homing In." *Recovering the Word: Essays on Native American Literature.* Ed. Brian Swann and Arnold Krupat. Berkeley: U of California P, 1987. 580–620.

Bhabha, Homi K. " 'Caliban Speaks to Prospero': Cultural Identity and the Crisis of Representation." Conference presentation. Dia Center for the Arts. *Critical Fictions: The Politics of Imaginative Writing.* Ed. Philomena Mariani. Seattle: Bay P, 1991. 62–65.

———. *The Location of Culture.* London: Routledge, 1994.

Bredin, Renae. " 'Becoming Minor': Reading *The Woman Who Owned the Shadows.*" *Studies in American Indian Literature* 6.4 (Winter 1994): 36–50.

Bringhurst, Robert. "That Also Is You: Some Classics of Native Canadian Literature." *Canadian Literature* 124–25 (Spring-Summer 1990): 32–47.

Brodribb, Somer. "The Traditional Roles of Native Women in Canada and the Impact of Colonization." *The Canadian Journal of Native Studies* 4.1 (1984): 85–103.

Brown, Alanna Kathleen. "Legacy Profile, Mourning Dove (Humishuma) (1888–1936)." *Legacy, A Journal of Nineteenth Century American Women Writers* 6.1 (Spring 1989): 51–58.

———. "Looking through the Glass Darkly: The Editorialized Mourning Dove." *New Voices in Native American Literary Criticism.* Ed. Arnold Krupat. Washington: Smithsonian Institution Press, 1993. 274–90.

———. "Mourning Dove, An Indian Novelist." *Plainswoman* 11.5 (January 1988): 3–4.

———. "Mourning Dove's Voice in *Cogewea.*" *The Wicazo Sa Review: A Journal of Indian Studies* 4.2 (Fall 1988): 2–15.

Brown, Jennifer S. H. "Woman as Center and Symbol in the Emergence of Metis Communities." *The Canadian Journal of Native Studies* 3.1 (1983): 39–46.

Bruchac, Joseph, ed. *Survival This Way: Interviews with American Indian Poets.* Tucson: Sun Tracks and U of Arizona P, 1987.

Brumble, H. David, III. *American Indian Autobiography.* Berkeley: U of California P, 1988.

Burt, Larry W. "In a Crooked Piece of Time: The Dilemma of the Montana Cree and the Metis." *Journal of American Culture* 9 (Spring 1986): 45–51.

Campbell, Maria. *Halfbreed.* Lincoln: U of Nebraska P, 1973.

Carr, Helen. *Inventing the American Primitive: Politics, Gender, and the Representation of Native American Literary Traditions, 1789–1936.* New York: New York UP, 1996.

Christian, Barbara. "Community and Nature: The Novels of Toni Morrison." *The Journal of Ethnic Studies* 7.4 (Winter 1980): 65–78.

———. "Fixing Methodologies: *Beloved.*" *Cultural Critique* 24 (Spring 1993): 5–15.

———. " 'Somebody Forgot to Tell Somebody Something': African American Women's Historical Novels." *Wild Women in the Whirlwind: Afra-American Culture and the Contemporary Literary Renaissance.* Ed. Joanne M. Braxton and Andrée Nicola McLaughlin. New Brunswick: Rutgers UP, 1990. 326–41.

Cixous, Hélène. *"Coming to Writing" and Other Essays.* Ed. Deborah Jensen. Cambridge: Harvard UP, 1991.

———. "Sorties: Out and Out: Attacks/Ways Out/Forays." In Cixous and Clément.

———. *Three Steps on the Ladder of Writing.* Trans. Sarah Cornell and Susan Sellers. The Wellek Library Lectures of the University of California, Irvine. New York: Columbia UP, 1993.

———. "We Who Are Free, Are We Truly Free?" Trans. Chris Miller. *Cultural Critique* 24: (Spring 1993): 201–19.

Cixous, Hélène, and Catherine Clément. *The Newly Born Woman.* Trans. Betsy Wing. Theory and History of Literature 24. Minneapolis: U of Minnesota P, 1986. 63–129.

Clifford, James. Introduction. "Partial Truths." *Writing Culture: The Poetics and Politics of Ethnography.* Ed. Clifford and George E. Marcus. Berkeley: U of California P, 1986. 1–26.

———. "Objects and Selves—An Afterword." *Objects and Others: Essays on Museums and Material Culture.* Ed. George W. Stocking, Jr. Madison: U of Wisconsin P, 1985. 236–45.

———. "On Ethnographic Allegory." *Writing Culture: The Poetics and Politics of Ethnography.* Ed. Clifford and Marcus. Berkeley: U of California P, 1986. 98–121.

———. "On Ethnographic Authority." *Representations* 1.2: 118–46.

———. *The Predicament of Culture: Twentieth-Century Ethnography, Literature, and Art.* Cambridge: Harvard UP, 1988.

Coltelli, Laura, ed. *Winged Words: American Indian Writers Speak.* Lincoln: U of Nebraska P, 1990.

Cornell, Drucilla. *Transformations: Recollective Imagination and Sexual Difference.* New York: Routledge, 1993.

Crawford, John F., and others, eds. *This Is about Vision: Interviews with Southwestern Writers.* New America Studies in the American West. Albuquerque: U of New Mexico P, 1990.

Culler, Jonathan. *On Deconstruction: Theory and Criticism After Structuralism.* Ithaca: Cornell UP, 1983.

Culleton, Beatrice. *In Search of April Raintree.* Winnipeg: Pemmican, 1983.

Currey, Noel Elizabeth. "Jeannette Armstrong and the Colonial Legacy." *Canadian Literature* 124-25 (Spring-Summer 1990): 138-52.

Dasenbrock, Reed Way. "Do We Write the Text We Read?" *College English* 53.1 (January 1991): 7-18.

Dearborn, Mary. *Pocahontas's Daughters: Gender and Ethnicity in American Culture.* New York: Oxford UP, 1986.

de Lauretis, Teresa. "Displacing Hegemonic Discourses: Reflections on Feminist Theory in the 1980s." *Inscriptions* 3 & 4 (1988): 127-44.

————. "Feminist Studies/Critical Studies: Issues, Terms, and Contexts." *Feminist Studies/Critical Studies.* Ed. de Lauretis. Bloomington: Indiana UP, 1986. 1-19.

Deloria, Vine. *Custer Died for Your Sins: An Indian Manifesto.* New York: Avon, 1969.

Devens, Carol. *Countering Colonization: Native American Women and Great Lakes Missions, 1630-1900.* Berkeley: U of California P, 1992.

di Leonardo, Micaela. "Gender, Culture, and Political Economy: Feminist Anthropology in Historical Perspective." *Gender at the Crossroads of Knowledge: Feminist Anthropology in the Post-Modern Era.* Ed. di Leonardo. Berkeley: U of California P, 1991.

Donaldson, Laura E. *Decolonizing Feminisms: Race, Gender and Empire Building.* Chapel Hill: U of North Carolina P, 1992.

Donovan, Josephine. "Style and Power." *Feminism, Bakhtin, and the Dialogic.* Ed. Dale M. Bauer and Susan Jaret McKinstry. Albany: State U of New York P, 1991. 85-94.

Douglas, Mary. *Purity and Danger: An Analysis of Concepts of Pollution and Taboo.* 1966. Boston: Routledge, 1980.

Driben, Paul. "The Nature of Metis Claims." *The Canadian Journal of Native Studies* 3.1 (1983): 183-96.

Enloe, Cynthia. *Bananas, Beaches and Bases: Making Feminist Sense of International Politics.* Berkeley: U of California P, 1989.

Erdrich, Louise. "Where I Ought To Be: A Writer's Sense of Place." *The New York Times Book Review* (28 July 1985): 1+.

Etienne, Mona, and Eleanor Burke Leacock, eds. *Women and Colonization: Anthropological Perspectives.* New York: Praeger, 1980.

Evans-Pritchard, E. E. *The Position of Women in Primitive Societies and Other Essays in Social Anthropology*. New York: Free P, 1965.

Evers, Larry. "Continuity and Change in American Indian Oral Literatures." *ADE Bulletin* 75 (Summer 1983): 43–66.

———. "Words and Place: A Reading of *House Made of Dawn*." *Western American Literature* 11 (February 1977): 297–320.

Evers, Larry, and Felipe Molina. *Yaqui Deer Songs / Maso Bwikam: A Native American Poetry*. Tucson: Sun Tracks and U of Arizona P, 1987.

Fabian, Johannes. *Time and the Other: How Anthropology Makes Its Object*. New York: Columbia UP, 1983.

Fanon, Franz. *The Wretched of the Earth*. Trans. Constance Farrington. New York: Grove Weidenfeld, 1963.

Fee, Margery. "Upsetting Fake Ideas: Jeanette Armstrong's 'Slash' and Beatrice Culleton's 'April Raintree.' *Canadian Literature* 124–25 (Spring-Summer 1990): 168–80.

Ferguson, Russell, ed. *Out There: Marginalization and Contemporary Cultures*. Cambridge: MIT P, 1990.

Fetterley, Judith. *The Resisting Reader: A Feminist Approach to American Fiction*. Bloomington: Indiana UP, 1978.

Finn, Janet L. "Ella Cara Deloria and Mourning Dove: Writing for Cultures, Writing against the Grain." *Critique of Anthropology* 13.4 (1993): 335–49.

Finnegan, Ruth. *Oral Poetry: Its Nature, Significance and Social Context*. Cambridge: Cambridge UP, 1977.

Fish, Stanley. *Is There a Text in This Class? The Authority of Interpretive Communities*. Cambridge: Harvard UP, 1980.

Fisher, Dexter. Introduction. *Cogewea, The Half-Blood: A Depiction of the Great Montana Cattle Range*. By Mourning Dove. Lincoln: U of Nebraska P, 1981.

———. "The Transformation of Tradition: A Study of Zitkala-Sa and Mourning Dove, Two Traditional Indian Writers." *Critical Essays on Native American Literature*. Ed. Andrew Wiget. Boston: G. K. Hall, 1985. 202–11.

Foucault, Michel. "What Is an Author?" *Contemporary Literary Criticism: Literary and Cultural Studies*. Ed. Robert Con Davis and Ronald Schleifer. 3rd ed. New York: Longman, 1994. 341–53.

Frideres, James S. *Canada's Indians: Contemporary Conflicts*. Scarborough, Ontario: Prentice-Hall, 1974.

Gal, Susan. "Between Speech and Silence: The Problematics of Research on Language and Gender." *Gender at the Crossroads of Knowledge: Feminist Anthropology in the Postmodern Era*. Ed. Micaela di Leonardo. Berkeley: U of California P, 1991. 175-203.

Gallop, Jane. *The Daughter's Seduction: Feminism and Psychoanalysis*. Ithaca: Cornell UP, 1982.

Gibbins, Roger. "Canadian Indian Policy: The Constitutional Trap. *The Canadian Journal of Native Studies* 4.1 (1984): 1-9.

Gibson, Donald. "Individualism and Community in Black History and Fiction." *Black American Literature Forum* 11.4 (Winter 1977): 123-29.

Goddard, Barbara. "The Politics of Representation: Some Native Canadian Women Writers." *Canadian Literature* 124-25 (Spring-Summer 1990): 183-225.

Goldman, Anna E. "Is That What She Said? The Politics of Collaborative Autobiography." *Cultural Critique* (Fall 1993): 177-204.

Gordon, Deborah. "Writing Culture, Writing Feminism: The Poetics and Politics of Experimental Ethnography." *Inscriptions* 3 and 4 (1988): 7-26.

Gormley, Daniel J. "Aboriginal Rights as Natural Rights." *The Canadian Journal of Native Studies* 4.1 (1984): 29-49.

Gould, Janice. *Earthquake Weather*. Tucson: Sun Tracks and the U of Arizona P, 1996.

Grant, Agnes. "Contemporary Native Women's Voices in Literature." *Canadian Literature* 124-125 (Spring-Summer 1990): 124-32.

Green, Rayna. "Native American Women." *Signs: Journal of Women in Culture and Society* 6 (Winter 1980): 248-67.

———. *Native American Women: A Contextual Bibliography*. Bloomington: Indiana UP, 1983.

Griffin, Susan. *Pornography and Silence: Culture's Revenge Against Nature*. New York: Harper Colophon, 1981.

Hanson, Elizabeth I. *Forever There: Race and Gender in Contemporary Native American Fiction*. American University Studies, Series XXIV, American Literature, v. 11. New York: Peter Lang, 1989.

Harjo, Joy. *In Mad Love and War*. Middletown, CT: Wesleyan UP, 1990.

———. "Ordinary Spirit." *I Tell You Now: Autobiographical Essays by Native American Writers*. Ed. Brian Swann and Arnold Krupat. Lincoln: U of Nebraska P, 1987. 263-70.

———. Interview in "Poetics and Politics: A Series of Readings by Native American Writers." U of Arizona. 27 April 1992.

———. *She Had Some Horses.* New York: Thunder's Mouth, 1983.

———. *The Woman Who Fell from the Sky.* New York: Norton, 1994.

Harjo, Joy, and Stephen Strom. *Secrets from the Center of the World.* Tucson: Sun Tracks and U of Arizona P, 1989.

Harrison, Julia D. *Metis: People Between Two Worlds.* Vancouver: Douglas and McIntyre, 1985.

Herndl, Diane Price. "The Dilemmas of a Feminine Dialogic." *Feminism, Bakhtin, and the Dialogic.* Ed. Dale M. Bauer and Jaret McKinstry. Albany: State U of New York P, 1991. 7–24.

Herzog, Kristin. *Women, Ethnics, and Exotics: Images of Power in Mid-Nineteenth Century American Fiction.* Knoxville: U of Tennessee P, 1983.

Hinton, Leanne. *Havasupai Songs: A Linguistic Perspective.* Tubingen: Narr, 1984.

Hinton, Leanne, and Lucille J. Watahomigie, eds. *Spirit Mountain: An Anthology of Yuman Story and Song.* Tucson: Sun Tracks and U of Arizona P, 1984.

hooks, bell [Gloria Watkins]. *Black Looks: Race and Representation.* Boston: South End, 1992.

———. *Talking Back: Thinking Feminist, Thinking Black.* Boston: South End, 1989.

———. *Yearning: Race, Gender, and Cultural Politics.* Boston: South End, 1990.

Hoy, Helen. " 'Nothing but the Truth': Discursive Transparency in Beatrice Culleton." *ARIEL: A Review of International English Literature* 25.1 (January 1994): 155–84.

Hunt, Patricia. "War and Peace: Transfigured Categories and the Politics of *Sula.*" *African American Review* 27.3 (Fall 1993): 443–60.

Huyssen, Andreas. "Mass Culture as Woman: Modernism's Other." *Studies in Entertainment: Critical Approaches to Mass Culture.* Ed. Tania Modleski. Bloomington: Indiana UP, 1986. 188–207.

Irigaray, Luce. *This Sex Which Is Not One.* Trans. Catherine Porter. Ithaca: Cornell UP, 1985.

Jaskoski, Helen. "A MELUS Interview: Joy Harjo." *MELUS* 16.1 (Spring 1989–90): 5–13.

————. " 'My Heart Will Go Out': Healing Songs of Native American Women." *International Journal of Women's Studies* 4.4 (1981): 118–34.

Johnson, Emily Pauline. *The Moccasin Maker.* 1913. Tucson: U of Arizona P, 1987.

Johnson-Odim, Cheryl. "Common Themes, Different Contexts: Third World Women and Feminism." *Third World Women and the Politics of Feminism.* Ed. Chandra Mohanty and others. Bloomington: Indiana UP, 1991. 314–27.

Johnston, Basil H. "One Generation from Extinction." *Canadian Literature* 124–25 (Spring–Summer 1990): 10–15.

Katz, Jane B. Introduction. *I Am the Fire of Time: The Voices of Native American Women.* New York: Dutton, 1977. xv–xix.

Kienetz, Alvin. "The Rise and Decline of Hybrid (Metis) Societies on the Frontier of Western Canada and Southern Africa." *The Canadian Journal of Native Studies* 3.1 (1983): 3–21.

King, Thomas, ed. *All My Relations: An Anthology of Contemporary Canadian Native Writing.* Toronto: McLelland and Stewart, 1990.

King, Thomas, Cheryl Calver, and Helen Hoy, eds. *The Native in Literature: Canadian and Comparative Perspectives.* Winnipeg: Hignell, 1987.

Kodish, Debora. "Absent Gender, Silent Encounter." *Journal of American Folklore* 100.398 (October-December 1987): 573–78.

Kolodny, Annette. *The Lay of the Land: Metaphor As Experience and History in American Life and Letters.* Chapel Hill: U of North Carolina P, 1975.

Kristeva, Julia. *Powers of Horror: An Essay on Abjection.* Trans. Leon S. Roudiez. New York: Columbia UP, 1982.

Kroeber, Karl. "American Ethnopoetics: A New Cultural Dimension." *Arizona Quarterly* 45.2 (Summer 1989): 1–13.

Krupat, Arnold, ed. *New Voices in Native American Literary Criticism.* Washington: Smithsonian Institution P, 1993.

————. *The Voice in the Margin: Native American Literature and the Canon.* Berkeley: U of California P, 1989.

Kulchyski, Peter. "Primitive Subversions: Totalization and Resistance in Native Canadian Politics." *Cultural Critique* 0882–4371 (Spring 1992): 171–95.

LaRoque, Emma. *Defeathering the Indian.* Agincourt: Book Society of Canada, 1975.

Larson, Charles E. *American Indian Fiction.* Albuquerque: U of New Mexico P, 1978.

Leacock, Eleanor Burke, and Mona Etienne, eds. *Women and Colonization: Anthropological Perspectives.* New York: Praeger, 1980.

Le Clair, Thomas. "The Language Must Not Sweat: A Conversation with Toni Morrison." *New Republic* (2 March 1981): 25–29.

Lee, Dorothy H. "The Quest for Self: Triumph and Failure in the Works of Toni Morrison." *Black Women Writers (1950–1980): A Critical Evaluation.* Ed. Mari Evans. Garden City: Anchor, 1984. 346–60.

Lee, Sky, and Lee Maracle, Daphne Marlatt, and Betsy Warland, eds. *Telling It: Women and Language Across Cultures.* Vancouver: Press Gang, 1990.

Lewis, Vashti Crutcher. "African Tradition in Toni Morrison's *Sula.*" *Wild Women in the Whirlwind: Afra-American Culture and the Contemporary Literary Renaissance.* Ed. Braxton and McLaughlin. New Brunswick: Rutgers UP, 1990. 316–25.

Limerick, Patricia Nelson. *The Legacy of Conquest: The Unbroken Past of the American West.* New York: Norton, 1987.

Lionnet, Françoise. *Autobiographical Voices: Race, Gender, Self-Portraiture.* Ithaca: Cornell UP, 1989.

Lorde, Audre. "Poetry Is Not a Luxury." *Sister Outsider: Essays and Speeches by Audre Lorde.* Freedom, CA: Crossing, 1984. 36–39.

Lounsberry, Barbara, and Grace Ann Hovet. "Principles of Perception in Toni Morrison's *Sula.*" *Black American Literature Forum* 13.4 (Winter 1979): 126–29.

Lugones, María C., and Elizabeth V. Spelman. "Have We Got a Theory for You! Feminist Theory, Cultural Imperialism, and the Demand for 'the Woman's Voice.' " *Hypatia Reborn: Essays in Feminist Philosophy.* Ed. Azizah Y. al-Hibri and Margaret A. Simons. Bloomington: Indiana UP, 1990. 18–33.

Lutz, Harmut, ed. *Contemporary Challenges: Conversations with Canadian Native Writers.* Saskatoon: Fifth House, 1991.

MacDonald, Mary Lu. "Red and White Men; Black, White and Grey Hats: Literary Attitudes to the Interaction between European and Native Canadians in the First Half of the Nineteenth Century." *Canadian Literature* 124–25 (Spring–Summer 1990): 92–111.

MacEwan, Grant. *Metis Makers of History.* Saskatoon: Western Producer Prairie Books, 1981.

Maracle, Lee. *Bobbi Lee, Indian Rebel: Struggles of a Native Canadian Woman.* Ed. Don Barnett. Richmond, B.C.: LSM, 1975.

————. *I Am Woman.* North Vancouver, B.C.: Write-On, 1988.

————. *Sojourner's Truth and Other Stories.* Vancouver, B.C.: Press Gang Publishers, 1990.

————. *Telling It: Women and Language Across Cultures.* Ed. The Telling It Book Collective. Vancouver, B.C.: Press Gang Publishers, 1990.

Mariani, Philomena, ed. *Critical Fictions: The Politics of Imaginative Writing.* Seattle: Bay Press, 1991.

Martin, Biddy, and Chandra Talpade Mohanty. "Feminist Politics: What's Home Got to Do with It?" *Feminist Studies/Critical Studies.* Ed. Teresa de Lauretis. Bloomington: Indiana UP, 1986. 191–212.

Menchú, Rigoberta. *I, Rigoberta Menchú: An Indian Woman in Guatemala.* Ed. Elisabeth Burgos-Debray. Trans. Ann Wright. London: Verso, 1984.

Miller, Jay, ed. *Mourning Dove: A Salishan Autobiography.* Lincoln: U of Nebraska P, 1990.

Miller, J. R. "From Riel to the Metis." *Canadian Historical Review* 69 (March 1988): 1–20.

Miller, Nancy K. "Changing the Subject: Authorship, Writing, and the Reader." *Feminist Studies/Critical Studies.* Ed. Teresa de Lauretis. Bloomington: Indiana UP, 1986. 102–20.

Mobley, Marilyn Sanders. *Folk Roots and Mythic Wings in Sarah Orne Jewett and Toni Morrison: The Cultural Function of Narrative.* Baton Rouge: Louisiana State UP, 1991.

Modeleski, Tania. "Feminism and the Power of Interpretation: Some Critical Readings." *Feminist Studies/Critical Studies.* Ed. Teresa de Lauretis. Bloomington: Indiana UP, 1986. 121–38.

Mohanty, Chandra Talpade. "Cartographies of Struggle: Third World Women and the Politics of Feminism." *Third World Women and the Politics of Feminism.* Ed. Mohanty, Ann Russo, and Lourdes Torres. Bloomington: Indiana UP, 1991. 1–50.

————. "Under Western Eyes: Feminist Scholarship and Colonial Discourses." *Third World Women and the Politics of Feminism.* Ed. Mohanty and others. Bloomington: Indiana UP, 1991. 51–80.

Mohanty, Satya P. "The Epistemic Status of Cultural Identity: On *Beloved* and the Postcolonial Condition." *Cultural Critique* 24 (Spring 1993): 41–80.

Moi, Toril. *Sexual/Textual Politics: Feminist Literary Theory.* London: Routledge, 1985.

Momaday, N. Scott. *The Ancient Child.* New York: Doubleday, 1989.

————. *House Made of Dawn.* New York: Harper and Row, 1966.

————. "The Man Made of Words." *The Remembered Earth: An Anthology of Contemporary Native American Literature.* Ed. Geary Hobson. Albuquerque: U of New Mexico P, 1980. 162–73.

Morisset, Jean. "Les Métis et L'Idée du Canada." *The Canadian Journal of Native Studies* 3.1 (1983): 197–213.

Morrison, Toni. *Beloved.* New York: New American Library, 1987.

————. *Jazz.* New York: Alfred A. Knopf, 1992.

————. *Playing in the Dark: Whiteness and the Literary Imagination.* The William E. Massey, Sr., Lectures in the History of American Civilization. Cambridge: Harvard UP, 1992.

————. "Rootedness: The Ancestor as Foundation." *Black Women Writers (1950–1980): A Critical Evaluation.* Ed. Mari Evans. Garden City: Anchor, 1984. 339–45.

————. *Sula.* New York: New American Library, 1973.

Mourning Dove. *Cogewea, The Half-Blood: A Depiction of the Great Montana Cattle Range.* 1927. Lincoln: U of Nebraska P, 1981.

————. *Coyote Stories.* 1933. Lincoln: U of Nebraska P, 1990.

————. *Mourning Dove: A Salishan Autobiography.* Ed. Jay Miller. Lincoln: U of Nebraska P, 1990.

Murphy, Patrick. "Prolegomenon for an Ecofeminist Dialogics." *Feminism, Bakhtin, and the Dialogic.* Ed. Dale M. Bauer and Susan Jaret McKinstry. Albany: State U of New York P, 1991. 39–56.

Murray, David. *Forked Tongues: Speech, Writing and Representation in North American Indian Texts.* Bloomington: Indiana UP, 1991.

Naranjo-Morse, Nora. *Mud Woman: Poems from the Clay.* Tucson: Sun Tracks and the U of Arizona P, 1992.

Ogunyemi, Chikwenye Okonjo. "*Sula:* 'A Nigger Joke.' " *Black American Literature Forum* 13.4 (Winter 1979): 130–33.

Okpewho, Isidore. *Myth in Africa: A Study of Its Aesthetic and Cultural Relevance.* Cambridge: Cambridge UP, 1983.

Ortiz, Simon J. *Woven Stone.* Tucson: Sun Tracks and U of Arizona P, 1992.

Ortner, Sherry. "Is Female to Male as Nature Is to Culture?" *Woman, Culture, and Society.* Ed. Michelle Zimbalist Rosaldo and Louise Lamphere. Stanford: Stanford UP, 1974. 67–87.

Pearlman, Mickey, ed. "Joy Harjo." *Listen to Their Voices: 20 Interviews with Women Who Write.* Boston: Houghton Mifflin, 1993. 91–98.

Person, Leland S., Jr. "The American Eve: Miscegenation and a Feminist Frontier Fiction." *American Quarterly* 37 (Winter 1985): 668–85.

Petrone, Penny. *Native Literature in Canada: From the Oral Tradition to the Present.* Toronto: Oxford UP, 1990.

Pike, Charles A. "Form and Memory in Oral Tradition." *Phenomenology in Modern African Studies.* Ed. Sunday O. Anozie. Buffalo: Conch Magazine, Ltd., 1982. 13–29.

"Poetics and Politics: A Series of Readings by Native American Writers." U of Arizona. 27 April 1992.

Price, John. *Indians of Canada: Cultural Dynamics.* Scarborough: Prentice-Hall, 1979.

Pratt, Mary Louise. "Fieldwork in Common Places." *Writing Culture: The Poetics and Politics of Ethnography.* Ed. James Clifford and George E. Marcus. Berkeley: U of California P, 1986. 27–50.

———. *Imperial Eyes: Travel Writing and Transculturation.* London: Routledge, 1992.

Radford-Hill, Sheila. "Considering Feminism as a Model for Social Change." *Feminist Studies/Critical Studies.* Ed. Teresa de Lauretis. Bloomington: Indiana UP, 1986. 157–72.

Radner, Joan N., and Susan S. Lanser. "The Feminist Voice: Strategies of Coding in Folklore and Literature." *Journal of American Folklore* 100 (1987): 412–25.

Rebolledo, Tey Diana. "The Politics of Poetics: Or, What Am I, A Critic, Doing in This Text Anyhow?" *Making Face, Making Soul/Haciendo Caras: Creative and Critical Perspectives by Women of Color.* Ed. Gloria Anzaldúa. San Francisco: Aunt Lute, 1990. 346–55.

Rich, Adrienne. *Blood, Bread, and Poetry: Selected Prose 1979–1985.* New York: Norton, 1986.

Root, Deborah. *Cannibal Culture: Art, Appropriation, and the Commodification of Difference.* Boulder, CO: Westview, 1996.

Rosaldo, Michelle Zimbalist. "A Theoretical Overview." *Woman, Culture, and Society.* Ed. Rosaldo and Louise Lamphere. Stanford: Stanford UP, 1974. 17–42.

Rosaldo, Renato. *Culture and Truth: The Remaking of Social Analysis.* Boston: Beacon, 1989.

———. "From the Door of His Tent: The Fieldworker and the Inquisitor." *Writing Culture: The Poetics and Politics of Ethnography.* Ed. James Clifford and George Marcus. Berkeley: U of California P, 1986. 77–97.

Ruoff, A. LaVonne Brown. Introduction. *The Moccasin Maker.* By Emily Pauline Johnson. 1913. Tucson: U of Arizona P, 1987. 1–37.

Said, Edward. *Culture and Imperialism.* New York: Knopf, 1993.

———. "Reflections on Exile." *Out There: Marginalization and Contemporary Cultures.* Ed. Russell Ferguson and others. Cambridge: MIT P, 1990. 357–66.

Saldívar, José David. *The Dialectics of Our America: Genealogy, Cultural Critique, and Literary History.* Durham: Duke UP, 1991.

Scarberry-García, Susan. *Landmarks of Healing: A Study of* House Made of Dawn. Albuquerque: U of New Mexico P, 1990.

Scheik, William J. *The Half-Blood: A Cultural Symbol in Nineteenth Century American Fiction.* Lexington: U of Kentucky P, 1979.

Schweickart, Patrocinio P. "Reading Ourselves: Toward a Feminist Theory of Reading." *Gender and Reading: Essays on Readers, Texts, and Contexts.* Ed. Elizabeth A. Flynn and Patrocinio P. Schweickart. Baltimore: Johns Hopkins UP, 1986. 31–62.

Schweickart, Patrocinio P., and Elizabeth A. Flynn. Introduction. *Gender and Reading: Essays on Readers, Texts, and Contexts.* Ed. Schweickart and Flynn. Baltimore: Johns Hopkins UP, 1986.

Shiach, Morag. *Hélène Cixous: A Politics of Writing.* London: Routledge, 1991.

Shreve, Gregory A. "Structure and Reference: A Theory of African Narrative." *Phenomenology in Modern African Studies.* Ed. Sunday O. Anozie. Buffalo: Conch Magazine, 1982. 31–47.

Silko, Leslie Marmon. *Almanac of the Dead.* New York: Simon and Schuster, 1991.

———. *Ceremony.* New York: Penguin, 1977.

———. "Landscape, History, and the Pueblo Imagination." *On Nature: Nature, Landscape, and Natural History.* Ed. Daniel Halpern. San Francisco: North Point, 1986. 83–94.

———. *Storyteller.* New York: Seaver, 1981.

Silver, A. I. "Ontario's Alleged Fanaticism in the Riel Affair." *Canadian Historical Review* 69 (March 1988): 21–50.

Slotkin, Richard. *Gunfighter Nation: The Myth of the Frontier in Twentieth-Century America.* New York: Atheneum, 1992.

Smith, Barbara Hernstein. *Contingencies of Value: Alternative Perspectives for Critical Theory.* Cambridge: Harvard UP, 1988.

Smithson, Carma Lee. "The Havasupai Woman." *University of Utah Anthro-pological Papers* 38 (April 1959).

Smithson, Carma Lee, and Robert C. Euler. "Havasupai Religion and My-thology." *University of Utah Anthropological Papers* 38 (April 1964).

Spier, Leslie. "Havasupai Ethnography." *Anthropological Papers of the American Museum of Natural History* 29–33 (1921).

Spivak, Gayatri Chakravorty. *In Other Worlds: Essays in Cultural Politics.* New York: Routledge, 1987.

———. *The Post-Colonial Critic: Interviews, Strategies, Dialogues.* Ed. Sarah Harasym. New York: Routledge, 1990.

Stallybrass, Peter, and Allon White. *The Politics and Poetics of Transgres-sion.* Ithaca: Cornell UP, 1986.

Stoler, Ann Laura. "Carnal Knowledge and Imperial Power: Gender, Race, and Morality in Colonial Asia." *Gender at the Crossroads of Knowl-edge: Feminist Anthropology in the Postmodern Era.* Ed. Micaela di Leonardo. Berkeley: U of California P, 1991. 51–101.

Suleiman, Susan. "Writing Past the Wall: or the Passion According to H. C." *"Coming to Writing" and Other Essays.* Ed. Deborah Jenson. Cam-bridge: Harvard UP, 1991.

Swann, Brian, and Arnold Krupat, eds. *I Tell You Now: Autobiographical Essays by Native American Writers.* Lincoln: U of Nebraska P, 1987.

Taylor, John Leonard. "An Historical Introduction to Metis Claims in Canada." *The Canadian Journal of Native Studies* 3.1 (1983): 151–81.

Tobique Women's Group. *Enough Is Enough: Aboriginal Women Speak Out.* Ed. Janet Silman. Toronto: Women's P, 1987.

Tompkins, Jane. *West of Everything: The Inner Life of Westerns.* New York: Oxford UP, 1992.

Trinh, T. Minh-ha. "Not You/Like You: Post Colonial Women and the Inter-locking Questions of Identity and Difference." *Making Face, Making Soul/Haciendo Caras: Creative and Critical Perspectives by Women of Color.* Ed. Gloria Anzaldúa. San Francisco: Aunt Lute, 1990. 371–75.

———. *When the Moon Waxes Red: Representation, Gender and Cultural Politics.* New York: Routledge, 1991.

———. *Woman, Native, Other: Writing Postcoloniality and Feminism.* Bloomington: Indiana UP, 1989.

Tuana, Nancy. "Re-fusing Nature/Nurture." *Hypatia Reborn: Essays in Femi-nist Philosophy.* Ed. Azizah Y. al-Hibri and Margaret A. Simons. Bloomington: Indiana UP, 1988. 70–89.

Turner, Bryan S. *The Body and Society: Explorations in Social Theory.* Oxford: Basil Blackwell, 1984.

Turner, Frederick Jackson. *The Significance of the Frontier in American History.* 1892. Ed. Harold P. Simonson. New York: Frederick Unger, 1963.

Vander, Judith. *Songprints: The Musical Experience of Five Shoshone Women.* Urbana: U of Illinois P, 1988.

Van Kirk, Sylvia. *Many Tender Ties: Women in Fur Trade Society, 1670–1870.* Norman: U of Oklahoma P, 1980.

Vizenor, Gerald. *Earthdivers: Tribal Narratives on Mixed Descent.* Minneapolis: U of Minnesota P, 1981.

White, Richard. " *'It's Your Misfortune and None of My Own': A History of the American West.* Norman: U of Oklahoma P, 1991.

Witherspoon, Gary. "Beautifying the World Through Art." *The South Corner of Time: Hopi, Navajo, Papago, Yaqui Tribal Literature.* Ed. Larry Evers. Tucson: Sun Tracks and U of Arizona P, 1980. 98–100.

Wong, Hertha Dawn. *Sending My Heart Back Across the Years: Tradition and Innovation in Native American Autobiography.* New York: Oxford UP, 1992.

Yellowknee, Clara. "Challenges Facing Native Women." Alberta Native Women's Conference. *First Report.* Edmonton: Alberta Native Women's Conference (1970): 10.

Zumthor, Paul. *Oral Poetry: An Introduction.* Trans. Kathryn Murphy-Judy. Minneapolis: U of Minnesota P, 1990.

INDEX

ABOUT THE AUTHOR

Kathleen M. Donovan is an assistant professor of English at South Dakota State University, where she teaches courses in contemporary American Indian literature, African American literature, multicultural literature, and women's literature. She received an M.A. in English from the University of Nebraska–Lincoln and a Ph.D. in English from the University of Arizona, with concentrations in Native American literature and critical theory. She has published essays on Native American literature in journals in the United States and Italy. Currently she is working on a book-length study of cinematic representations of Native American women.